# Quick and Easy Spanish Recipes

Simone and Inés Ortega

# Quick and Easy Spanish Recipes

# Introduction

In 1972, mother and daughter Simone and Inés Ortega published *1080 Recipes*—a comprehensive guide to Spanish cooking, and since then, it has become the bestselling Spanish cookbook of all time. It sold over three million copies and has been translated into multiple languages as the definitive source on Spanish cuisine.

Spanish cuisine refers to culinary traditions of Spain, as opposed to those of Latin America. Traditional Spanish cooking, at its heart, is straightforward and unfussy. Long before it became trendy to use fresh, seasonal, local produce, Spanish cooks were already practitioners of this approach. Eating in Spain has always been a shared experience— a time to gather around a table and to come together; it is, almost without exception, a social occasion.

This practice of breaking bread together with friends and family is so inherent in Spain that many dishes are made for a crowd in a big pot. Paella is named for the wide, flat pan in which it is cooked. Cazuela, the terracotta casserole dish and stew of the same name, is placed in the middle of the table with spoons.

The recipes in this book, culled from the Ortegas' seminal work, offer delicious and approachable meals for today's kitchen table. The authors take you by the hand on a journey around Spain, giving a genuine glimpse into the homes of a country where a love of good food and honest cooking is ever-present.

*¡Buen provecho!*

# Small Plates

When it comes to the art of kicking off a meal, the Spanish have it covered, and tapas—bite-sized morsels of food paired with a drink—are so delicious they often comprise an entire meal. "Tapa" comes from the word meaning lid or cover, which back in the day were needed over drinks to prevent flies from getting in. What started as a humble disk of bread has since evolved to wedges of Manchego cheese topped with membranillo (quince paste), slivers of Iberian ham, Basque country's crab-topped pintxos (open-face finger sandwiches), and olive caviar, just to name a few tapas. Served as a generous spread, tapas comprise the ultimate Spanish party, a time to gather and delight in the convivial nature of eating.

# Crab Tapa

*Makes 18*
*Cook time: 15 minutes*

— Generous ¾ cup (175 g/6oz crab) canned crabmeat, drained and shredded
— 6 tablespoons mayonnaise, homemade (page 230) or purchased
— 6 romaine lettuce leaves, finely shredded
— salt and pepper
— 3½ tablespoons (53 g) butter, at room temperature
— 18 slices baguette
— 3 eggs, hard-boiled (see page 230) and peeled

*For the garnishes*
— 4 tomatoes, seeded and finely chopped
— 10 pitted (stoned) black olives, sliced
— 4 gherkin pickles, drained and finely chopped

Put crabmeat in a bowl and beat in mayonnaise, then stir in lettuce. Season with salt and pepper.

Spread a little butter on one side of each slice of bread, taking care not to tear it, then top with crab mixture.

Slice egg into at least 6 slices each. Put an egg slice on top of each tapa, then garnish the tapa with tomatoes, black olives, and gherkins. Serve immediately or the bread will become soggy.

Pinchos de atún, tomate y espárrago

# Tuna, Tomato, and Asparagus Pinchos

*Makes 12*
*Cook time: 5 minutes*

— 1 large tomato, sliced
— 12 slices baguette, about ½ inch/
  1 cm thick
— 7 oz/200 g canned tuna, drained
  and flaked
— 12 jarred or blanched asparagus
  tips, drained and patted dry

Put a sliced tomato on top of each slice of bread, then top with some tuna and an asparagus tip. Serve immediately or the bread will become soggy.

# Curd Cheese and Goat Cheese Pastries

*Makes 12*
*Cook time: 25 minutes*

— 5 oz/150 g goat cheese, crumbled
— Generous 1 cup (6 oz/170 g) farmer
   cheese or similar
— 3 eggs
— salt and pepper
— 1 sheet puff pastry, thawed if frozen

Preheat the oven to 425°F/200°C/Gas Mark 6. Put goat cheese into a bowl, then mix in the curd cheese and eggs and season with salt and pepper.

Use a knife to cut pastry into twelve 2-inch (5 cm) squares or use a 2-inch (5 cm) round cookie cutter to cut out 12 rounds. Turn up the edges of each piece to make a little tart shape, or use them to line small tartlet pans.

Put pastries on a baking sheet and prick the bottom of each. Bake for 8 minutes, then remove and fill each one with cheese mixture. Return them to the oven and continue baking for 10 minutes, or until well risen and golden brown. Serve hot.

# Cheese and Ham Magdalenas

*Makes 12*
*Cook time: 25 minutes*

— 2 eggs
— 3½ tablespoons ( 53 g) butter
— 4 tablespoons grated cheese, such as Gruyère
— 3 heaping tablespoons all-purpose (plain) flour
— 1 teaspoon baking powder
— 3½ oz/100 g Serrano ham, finely chopped

Preheat the oven to 400°F/180°C/Gas Mark 4. Line 12 cups of a muffin tin with paper liners (cupcake cases).

Beat eggs in a bowl with a fork. Gently melt butter in a small pan, then add eggs. Immediately stir in cheese, flour, baking powder, and ham. Spoon this mixture into the muffin cups.

Bake magdalenas for 20 minutes, or until they begin to brown. Remove from oven and immediately remove them from the muffin tin. These are best when served recently baked and slightly warm.

# Ham and Egg Tapa

*Makes 24*
*Cook time: 15 minutes*

— 12 large slices bread
— 12 thin slices Serrano ham
— 5 tablespoons (75 g) butter or
  margarine, at room temperature, plus
  more (optional) for garnish
— chopped parsley, to garnish
— 4 eggs, hard-boiled (see page 230) and
  sliced into 6 rounds

Using a 2-inch (5 cm) round cookie cutter, cut out 24 rounds from the bread. Using the same cutter, cut out 24 rounds of ham. Butter one side of each slice of bread, taking care not to tear the bread. Sprinkle parsley over buttered side of each round, then top each with a round of ham.

Put an egg slice on top of each tapa, cut side down, then sprinkle with parsley. The tapas can be served like this, or you can pipe softened butter all around for a garnish, if you like. They are best served immediately, but if prepared in advance, store in the refrigerator until ready to serve.

# Soft Cheese Sandwiches

*Makes 20*
*Cook time: 10 minutes*

— scant ½ cup (100 g) ricotta cheese
— scant ½ cup (100 g) mascarpone
  cheese
— 2 tablespoons heavy (double) cream
— 1 teaspoon finely chopped chives,
  shallot, or scallion (spring onion)
— 10 slices white bread
— 10 slices rye bread

Beat together cheeses until combined, then beat in cream. Stir in chives. Remove the crusts from the bread. Spread mixture onto the slices of white bread and place slices of rye bread on top. Cut each sandwich diagonally in half to form two triangles. The sandwiches may be kept in the refrigerator for a short time before serving.

# Baked Cheese Sticks

*Makes about 20*
*Cook time: 20 minutes*

— 7 tablespoons (100 g) butter
— ¾ cup (95 g) all-purpose (plain) flour
— 1 cup (100 g) Parmesan cheese, grated
— salt (optional)
— 1 cup (50 g) bread crumbs (made from day-old bread)

Preheat the oven to 400°F/200°C/Gas Mark 6. Melt butter in a saucepan over low heat but do not allow it to brown. Remove pan from heat, stir in flour, then Parmesan. Season with salt, if you wish.

Spread bread crumbs out in a shallow dish. Shape scoops of the cheese mixture into long, fat sticks, about the size of your little finger. Roll the cheese sticks in bread crumbs and place on a baking sheet.

Bake for 8–10 minutes, until golden brown. Carefully transfer cheese sticks to a wire rack (they will break easily) and let cool completely before serving.

# Bread with Tomato

*Makes 8*
*Cook time: 10 minutes*

— 4 slices bread (from a large loaf)
— 1 large clove garlic, halved (optional)
— 1 large juicy tomato, halved
— extra-virgin olive oil, to drizzle
— salt
— 4 slices Serrano ham, halved
— 8 oil-packed anchovy fillets, well drained

Preheat the broiler (grill) to high.

Toast bread on both sides for 2 minutes, or until golden and crisp. Rub toast with the garlic clove, if you like, then rub cut sides of the tomato halves over the pieces of toast, pressing down, until only the skins remain. Drizzle some oil over each toast and sprinkle with a pinch of salt. Cut each slice of toast in half and top each half with a piece of ham and an anchovy fillet.

Serve immediately or the toasts will get soggy.

# Prunes with Roquefort, Raisins, and Pine Nuts

*Makes 12*
*Cook time: 10 minutes*

— 3.5 oz/100 g Roquefort cheese
— 3 tablespoons pine nuts
— 4 tablespoons raisins
— 1 tablespoon Malaga wine or
  sweet sherry
— 4 tablespoons half-and-half
  (single cream)
— 12 pitted prunes

Crumble Roquefort into a bowl and mash lightly with a fork. Add pine nuts, raisins, wine, and cream and mix to a paste. Spoon the paste inside prunes and secure prunes with a toothpick (cocktail stick). Put prunes on a plate and chill before serving.

# Fried Date and Bacon Pinchos

*Makes 20*
*Cook time: 25 minutes*

— 20 dates, pitted
— 20 thin slices (rashers) bacon
— 2–3 tablespoons peanut oil

Wrap each date with a slice (rasher) of bacon and secure with a toothpick (cocktail stick). Heat oil in a frying pan over medium heat. Add wrapped dates and cook, turning occasionally, for about 10 minutes, or until bacon is cooked through and lightly browned. Drain well and serve hot.

# Melon Balls with Ham

*Makes 24–36*
*Cook time: 10 minutes*

— 12 thin slices Serrano ham
— 1 melon, such as cantaloupe,
   halved and seeded

Depending on the width of the slices of ham, cut them into 2–3 slices lengthwise. Using a melon baller, cut 24–36 balls from the melon flesh. Wrap each ball in a piece of ham and secure the ends with a toothpick (cocktail stick); this makes the melon balls easier to pick up and eat.

# Olive Caviar

*Serves 8*
*Cook time: 5 minutes*

— 1¼ cups (5 oz/150 g) black olives, pitted
— 4 oil-packed anchovy fillets, well drained
— 1½ tablespoons capers, rinsed
— 2 tablespoons olive oil
— toast or savory crackers, to serve

Put olives, anchovies, and capers in a blender or food processor and process until they form a paste. Transfer to a bowl and slowly beat in oil.

Cover with plastic wrap (clingfilm) and store in the refrigerator until ready to use. Serve spread on toast or savory crackers. This spread will keep for up to 1 week when stored covered in the refrigerator.

# Asparagus, Ham, and Mayonnaise Tapa

*Makes 24*
*Cook time: 15 minutes*

— 24 fresh, jarred, or canned asparagus tips
— 12 thin slices cooked or cured ham
— 24 slices baguette
— ⅓ cup (75 g) mayonnaise, homemade (page 230) or purchased
— 2 jarred roasted red peppers, drained and thinly sliced

Preheat the broiler (grill) to high.

If using fresh asparagus tips, steam them for 3–5 minutes, or until tender, then cool completely in an ice bath. If using jarred or canned, rinse well.

Using decorative cookie cutters, cut out 24 shapes from ham slices.

Toast the bread under the broiler for 2 minutes on each side, or until golden brown. Use the same cutters to cut out 24 shapes from toast. Top toast shapes with pieces of ham, spread each one with a little mayonnaise, then put an asparagus tip in the center of each. Add a roasted pepper slice or two to each tapa. Secure with toothpicks and serve immediately or the toast will become soggy.

# Salads

Spain grows a cornucopia of fantastic fresh produce,
and salads and vegetables are nearly always served
as an appetizer or on their own. Often they are more
than the sum of their parts—who could resist roasted
red peppers and anchovies, or crunchy lettuce
hearts with hazelnuts and a creamy dressing, or the
Moroccan-influenced carrot and orange salad. These are
uncomplicated plates with ingredients that simply sing.

# Avocado and Shrimp (Prawn) Salad

*Serves 4*
*Cook time: 10 minutes*

— 4 avocados
— juice of ½ lemon, strained
— 3 tablespoons mayonnaise, homemade
  (page 230) or purchased
— 1 teaspoon capers, rinsed
— 4 tablespoons (2 oz/50 g) jarred salmon
  roe (keta caviar), drained
— 5 oz/150 g cooked shrimp (prawns),
  peeled

Halve, pit, and peel avocados, then cut the flesh into cubes. Put them in a bowl and sprinkle lemon juice over them. Stir in mayonnaise and capers. Transfer to a serving bowl and garnish with salmon roe and shrimp.

# Lettuce Heart Salad

*Serves 6*
*Cook time: 30 minutes*

*For the vinaigrette*
— 1 tablespoon white wine vinegar
— salt
— 3 tablespoons extra-virgin olive oil

*For the salad*
— 3 lettuce hearts, halved, rinsed,
 and patted dry
— 4 tablespoons cold half-and-half
 (single cream)
— 1 tablespoon Dijon mustard
— 1 tablespoon chopped toasted
 hazelnuts

To make the vinaigrette, beat vinegar with a pinch of salt in a bowl with a fork, then beat in oil.

To assemble the salad: Put lettuce hearts in a deep dish and pour vinaigrette over them. Let marinate for about 25 minutes, turning them from time to time.

Before serving, drain off vinaigrette and place a halved lettuce heart onto each plate. Mix cream, straight from the refrigerator, with a little mustard to taste, then pour it over the lettuce. Sprinkle with hazelnuts and serve.

Note: As a variation, prepare as above, but instead of using cream, cover lettuce hearts with semiliquid mayonnaise mixed with mashed anchovy fillets. This version can also be served with chopped hazelnuts on top.

# Carrot Salad with Orange

*Serves 4*
*Cook time: 10 minutes*

— 2 oranges
— 1 bunch (500 g) carrots, roughly grated

*For the dressing*
— juice of 1 lemon, strained
— 1 tablespoon orange blossom water
— 1 tablespoon powdered (icing) sugar
— salt

Peel oranges, then carefully remove pith and slice fruit. Put them into a bowl with the carrots.

To make the dressing, beat lemon juice, orange blossom water, and sugar with salt. Pour dressing over oranges and carrots, then cover and chill until serving.

# Egg Salad

*Serves 4*
*Cook time: 20 minutes*

— 5 oz/150 g fresh, jarred, or canned
   asparagus tips
— 7 oz/200 g green beans, trimmed
— 1 head of romaine lettuce, separated
   into leaves, or 6 cups mixed salad
   greens, rinsed and patted dry
— 4 eggs, hard-boiled (see page 230),
   quartered
— 4 tablespoons olive oil
— 4 slices bread
— 4 slices (rashers) bacon
— 2 tablespoons white vinegar
— 4 teaspoons honey
— salt and pepper

If using fresh asparagus tips, steam them for 3–5 minutes, or until tender, then cool completely in an ice bath. If using jarred or canned, rinse well.

Bring a saucepan of salted water to a boil. Add green beans and cook for 10 minutes, or until just tender. Drain them and then run under cold running water to cool. Drain again and transfer to a salad bowl. Add lettuce, eggs, and asparagus tips to the bowl. Set aside.

Heat oil in a large frying pan over medium heat. Add bread and pan-fry until golden on both sides. Remove, cut into pieces, and set aside.

Return pan to heat, add bacon, and fry until crispy. Cut bacon into pieces. Pour oil from pan into a small bowl and mix with vinegar and honey. Add a pinch of salt and pepper.

Add fried bread and bacon to salad bowl. Pour dressing over salad, toss, and serve.

# Red Bell Pepper, Egg, and Anchovy Salad

*Serves 6–8*
*Cook time: 5 minutes*

*For the dressing*
— 3 oil-packed anchovy fillets, well
  drained and chopped
— 4 tablespoons extra-virgin olive oil
— 1 tablespoon lemon juice
— pepper

*For the salad*
— 1 (12 oz/350 g) jar roasted red
  peppers, drained and sliced
— 1½ lb/700 g tomatoes, peeled, seeded,
  and quartered
— 4 eggs, hard-boiled (see page 230),
  peeled, and quartered
— 1⅔ cups (7 oz/200 g) black olives,
  pitted
— 6 oil-packed anchovy fillets, well
  drained, to garnish

To make the dressing, crush anchovies in a mortar with a pestle, then add oil, lemon juice, and pepper to taste and mix together. Set aside.

To assemble the salad, put roasted peppers, tomatoes, eggs, and olives in a salad bowl. Mix the dressing again, pour it over salad, and gently mix together. Garnish with the whole anchovy fillets and serve.

# Radish Salad

*Serves 6*
*Cook time: 5 minutes*

*For the dressing*
— generous ½ cup (5 oz/150 g) plain
  (natural) yogurt
— 1 tablespoon chopped scallions
  (spring onions)
— 1 tablespoon lemon juice
— salt and pepper

*For the salad*
— 11 oz/300 g mixed salad greens, such
  as lettuce, arugula (rocket), chicory,
  and radicchio, rinsed and patted dry
— ½ bunch radishes, thinly sliced

To make the dressing, beat yogurt, scallions (spring onions), and lemon juice in a bowl and season with salt and pepper. Cover and chill until serving.

To assemble the salad, mix salad greens and radishes together in a salad bowl. Pour the dressing over it and serve.

Note: You can give this salad a personal touch by adding various herbs, such as parsley, mint, basil, or chives. Cubes of apple are also delicious. A little mustard or some chopped herbs can also be added to the dressing.

# Russian Salad

*Serves 6–8*
*Cook time: 5 minutes*

— 9 oz/250 g potatoes, diced and cooked
  in boiling water until tender
— 1 bunch (17½ oz/500 g) carrots, diced
  and cooked in boiling water until
  tender
— 2¼ lb (1 kg) fresh peas, blanched
— 1 cup (230 g) mayonnaise, homemade
  (page 230) or purchased
— breadsticks, to serve

Drain vegetables, transfer to a bowl and
let cool.

Add mayonnaise and toss to combine thoroughly.
Refrigerate until ready to serve. Before serving,
stick a few breadsticks into
the salad.

Note: This is the classic version of Russian
salad. Delicious variations include adding pieces
of tart apple, walnut, or celery to the vegetables.
Cooked, peeled shrimp (prawns) also add an
exquisite flavor to a simple Russian salad.

# Artichoke, Potato, and Shrimp (Prawn) Salad

*Serves 6*
*Cook time: 20 minutes*

*For the dressing*
— 1 tablespoon tarragon vinegar
— 1 tablespoon lemon juice, strained
— 3 tablespoons olive oil
— 1 shallot, chopped
— 1 tablespoon chopped parsley
— salt and pepper

*For the salad*
— 8 frozen artichoke hearts
— 1½ lb (700 g) potatoes, quartered
— 2 tablespoons olive oil
— ½ lb/225 g (10/12 count) jumbo
   shrimp (king prawns), peeled with
   tails left on
— 1 small head lettuce, leaves separated,
   rinsed and patted dry

To make the dressing, beat together vinegar, lemon juice, oil, shallot, and parsley with a fork. Season with salt and pepper. Set aside.

To make the salad, bring a large pot of water to a boil. Add artichokes and potatoes and cook until tender. Drain. When vegetables are cool enough to handle, thickly slice potatoes and cut each artichoke into quarters.

Meanwhile, heat oil in a frying pan over medium heat. Add shrimp and pan-fry, stirring, for 3–5 minutes, until opaque.

Cut lettuce leaves into wide strips and use them to line the bottom and sides of a salad bowl. Add potatoes and artichoke hearts. Add shrimp and the oil they were cooked in. Pour dressing over the salad and toss. Serve while still warm.

# Navy (Haricot) Bean Salad

*Serves 6*
*Cook time: 5 minutes*

— 4½ cups (800 g) cooked navy (haricot) beans or 3 (14 oz/395 g) cans, drained
— 3 tablespoons white wine vinegar
— salt
— ⅔ cup (165 ml) sunflower oil
— 1 teaspoon chopped parsley
— 1 tablespoon finely chopped onion
— tomato slices, for serving

Put beans in a salad bowl. Whisk vinegar with a pinch of salt in another bowl, then whisk in oil. Pour dressing over beans, add parsley and onion, and toss lightly to mix. Garnish with tomato slices, if you like, and serve.

# Orange, Fennel, and Onion Salad

*Serves 6–8*
*Cook time: 10 minutes*

— 1 bulb (1 lb 5 oz/600 g) fennel,
  trimmed and halved lengthwise
— 3 large oranges
— 5 tablespoons olive oil
— 2 tablespoons fresh lemon juice
— salt and pepper
— 1 small onion, thinly sliced
— handful of black olives, pitted and
  sliced
— mint leaves, to garnish (optional)

Bring a saucepan of salted water to a boil. Add fennel, bring back to a boil, and cook for 2 minutes, then drain. When fennel is cool enough to handle, thickly slice it and set aside.

Peel oranges, removing any traces of white pith and thinly slice crosswise, reserving any juices in a large bowl.

To make the dressing, add olive oil and lemon juice to orange juice and whisk together with a fork. Season with salt and pepper.

Add fennel, oranges, onion, and olives to the bowl and gently toss together. Just before serving, pour the dressing over salad and toss gently. Garnish with mint leaves, if desired.

# Salad with Asparagus, York Ham, and Mayonnaise

*Serves 6*
*Cook time: 15 minutes (plus chilling time)*

— 1 bunch fresh white asparagus or
   1 can (14 oz/400 g) white asparagus
— 3 firm tomatoes
— salt
— 1 cucumber
— 3 eggs, hard-boiled (see page 230)
— 7 oz/200 g York or other cooked ham,
   diced
— 1 tablespoon chopped onion
— 1 tablespoon chopped parsley
— 4 tablespoons mayonnaise, homemade
   (page 230) or purchased

If using fresh asparagus, trim, peel, and cook in boiling water until slightly tender, 3 minutes. Drain the cooked (or canned) asparagus well and leave on a clean tea towel to dry.

Dice tomatoes, put them in a colander, sprinkle with a little salt and leave to drain.
Peel and dice cucumber, put it in another colander, sprinkle with salt, and leave to drain. Rinse both ingredients and pat dry.

Cut asparagus spears into 1-inch/2.5 cm lengths. Chop 1½ hard-boiled eggs and slice remaining eggs.

Mix together the asparagus, tomato, cucumber, chopped eggs, ham, onion, and half the parsley in a bowl. Stir in mayonnaise, cover, and chill in the refrigerator for 1 hour.

To serve, garnish the salad with sliced eggs and sprinkle with remaining parsley.

*Ensalada de garbanzos*

# Chickpea Salad

*Serves 4–6*
*Cook time: 10 minutes*

— 5 (14 oz/395 g) cans chickpeas
— 2 eggs, hard-boiled (see page 230),
   peeled and chopped
— salt

*For the dressing*
— 3 tablespoons white wine vinegar
— ½ cup plus 1 tablespoon (135 ml)
   extra-virgin olive oil
— 1 teaspoon chopped parsley
— 1 teaspoon chopped onion
— salt and pepper

To make the dressing, beat together the vinegar, oil, parsley, and onion, with a fork in a serving bowl. Season with salt and pepper.

Stir in chickpeas, then add eggs, gently mixing together. Season to taste with salt. Serve warm or cold.

# Rice

Rice, the cornerstone of Spanish home cooking, is grown principally in the Albufera wetlands of Valencia, but also as far south as Murcia and as far north as Pals, near the Costa Brava. What distinguishes Spanish rice from its risotto cousin is its plump yet firm texture, which allows the grain to absorb loads of flavor without turning mushy. Spanish rice is taut and chewy, most famous as paella and arroz negro (black rice), cooked with cuttlefish ink. Here you will also find vegetarian soupy rice with Swiss chard and haricot beans, a perfect winter warmer.

# Rice with Mushrooms and Sherry Sauce

*Serves 6*
*Cook time: 25 minutes*

— 2¾ cups (500 g/18 oz) quick-cooking rice
— juice of 1 lemon, strained
— 1 lb 10 oz/750 g mushrooms
— 4 tablespoons (60 g) butter
— 3 tablespoons olive oil
— 3 tablespoons all-purpose (plain) flour
— ¾ cup/175 ml good-quality dry sherry
— salt and pepper

Bring rice and 2¾ cups/650 ml water to a boil, cover, remove from heat, and set aside.

Fill a bowl with water and half the lemon juice. Clean mushrooms with lemon water; drain and chop the caps and stems.

Melt 2 tablespoons of butter in a large frying pan over low heat. Add mushrooms and the remaining lemon juice and fry, stirring occasionally, for about 6 minutes. Set aside.

Melt remaining butter in another pan with 1 tablespoon of oil. Gradually add flour, stirring constantly, sherry and 1½ cups/350 ml water. Let thicken; season with salt and pepper. Add mushrooms and juices, stir, reduce heat, and simmer for 5 minutes.

Meanwhile, heat remaining oil in a large pan over high heat. Add rice, season with salt, and stir until hot and coated in oil. Spoon rice into 6 individual molds; flip each mold onto a warm plate. Spoon mushrooms around the rice or serve mushrooms with rice on the side.

# Rice with Vegetables

*Serves 6*
*Cook time: 20 minutes*

— ¾ cup (175 ml) sunflower oil
— 3 large canned artichoke hearts
— 2 tomatoes, peeled, seeded, and chopped
— 1 onion, finely chopped
— 2 red bell peppers, chopped
— 1 clove garlic, peeled
— 1 sprig parsley, plus chopped parsley (optional) for garnish
— 8 almonds
— 3½ oz/100 g green beans, trimmed and chopped
— 3½ oz/100 g shelled fava (broad) beans (⅓ cup)
— 2 carrots, peeled and sliced
— 2 ½ cups (260 g) quick-cooking rice
— 2 ½ cups/590 ml vegetable stock or water
— pinch of saffron strands
— salt
— 2 eggs, hard-boiled (see page 230), peeled and sliced, to garnish (optional)

Heat a little of the oil in a frying pan over medium-high heat. Add artichokes and pan-fry until golden. Set aside.

Heat remaining oil in a Dutch oven (casserole) over medium-high heat. Add tomatoes, onion, and bell peppers and pan-fry, stirring occasionally, until browned.

Meanwhile, crush garlic, parsley sprig, and almonds in a large mortar.

When vegetables have browned, stir in the garlic mixture, along with green beans, fava beans, carrots, rice, stock, and saffron and season with salt. Bring to a boil, cover, reduce heat to low, and cook for 5 minutes, or until rice is tender. Remove from heat, cover, and let stand 5 minutes more.

Arrange the fried artichoke pieces on top, re-cover the pan, and let rest for 5 minutes. Serve garnished with chopped parsley and slices of hard-boiled egg, if desired.

Rice

# Black Rice

*Serves 6*
*Cook time: 30 minutes*

— 6 cups (1.5 L) fish stock, homemade
  or made with a stock cube
— 2 cups (1 lb 2 oz/500 g) paella
  (medium-grain) rice
— 14 oz/400 g small squid, cleaned
  (ink sacs reserved)
— 1 cup plus 2 tablespoons
  (275 ml/9 fl oz) olive oil
— 2 cloves garlic, finely chopped
— 3 tomatoes, peeled, seeded, and
  chopped
— 1 jarred roasted red pepper,
  drained and cut into strips
— salt

Bring fish stock to a simmer. Begin cooking rice in 4 cups/1 L of simmering stock over medium-low heat, covered.

Meanwhile, put squid ink sacs in a bowl of water. Using a sharp knife, cut squid bodies into thin rings. Reserve tentacles if planning on using.

Heat oil in a flameproof earthenware pot, a paella pan, or a large heavy-based frying pan over high heat. Add squid rings (and tentacles if you like) and cook, stirring frequently, for 3 minutes. Stir in garlic, tomatoes, and a generous ½ cup/150 ml of the stock. Reduce heat to medium-low, cover, and cook for 10 minutes.

Meanwhile, carefully remove ink sacs from the bowl of water and break them into a measuring cup (measuring jug). Add enough of remaining stock to make 5 cups/1.2 L.

After rice is cooked about halfway (10 minutes), add squid, tomatoes, squid ink liquid, roasted pepper strips, and salt. Cook until rice is completely cooked, about 10 more minutes. Let stand for 5 minutes, covered, before serving.

# Rice with Chicken and Green Beans

*Serves 8*
*Cook time: 25 minutes*

— ¾ cup/175 ml sunflower oil
— 1 (4½ lb/2 kg) chicken, cut into serving pieces
— ½ lb/250 g green beans, trimmed and chopped
— 5 oz/150 g tomatoes, peeled, seeded, and chopped
— 1 teaspoon paprika
— 2½ cups (250 g) quick-cooking rice
— pinch of saffron strands dissolved in 1 tablespoon hot water
— salt

Heat oil in a heavy-based pan over medium-high heat. Add chicken pieces and pan-fry for about 12 minutes, or until they are golden all over. Add beans and tomatoes and cook for 5 minutes. Sprinkle paprika over the top and stir in rice. Pour in 2¼ cups/530 ml water and add saffron. Season with salt and bring to a boil. Reduce to a low simmer and cook for 6 minutes uncovered. Remove from heat, cover, and let stand for 5 minutes before serving.

# Paella

*Serves 6–8*
*Cook time: 30 minutes*

— 2 ¼ lb/1 kg mussels, debearded or 1 lb
  2 oz/500 hardshell clams, scrubbed
— 2 ¼ cups/535 ml fish stock
— 2 chicken stock cubes
— ¾ cup (175 ml) olive oil
— 1 small onion, finely chopped
— 1 clove garlic, finely chopped
— 3 tablespoons tomato sauce or 1 large
  tomato, chopped
— ¾ lb/340 g cooked shrimp (prawns)
— 2¾ cups (300 g) quick-cooking rice
— salt
— 3 sprigs parsley
— pinch of saffron threads
— ⅔ cup (100 g) canned peas, drained
— 1 red bell pepper, cut into strips
— lemon wedges, to serve

Discard any shellfish with broken shells or any that do not shut when sharply tapped. Preheat oven to 350°F/180°C/Gas Mark 4. Gently heat stock and chicken stock cubes, but do not allow to boil.

Add enough oil to a paella pan or large, ovenproof frying pan to cover the bottom over medium-high heat. Add onion and garlic and cook, stirring, for 5 minutes, or until lightly browned. Add tomato sauce and cook, stirring, for a few minutes. Set aside a few shrimp and add the remaining shrimp with rice to the pan. Cook, stirring, for a few minutes. Nestle mussels or clams into rice. Season with a pinch of salt and pour in stock. Gently shake the pan to evenly distribute liquid.

Pound parsley with saffron, and add to the pan with 2 tablespoons of water; gently shake or stir. Add peas and cook a few minutes; clams or mussels should open by then (discard any that do not). Top paella with pepper and reserved shrimp. Transfer pan to the oven for 20 minutes. Remove pan from the oven and let stand for 5 minutes. Serve with lemon wedges.

# Rice with Ham and Chorizo

*Serves 6*
*Cook time: 20 minutes*

— 3 cups (320 g) quick-cooking rice
— 3 tablespoons sunflower oil
— 1 onion, finely chopped
— 3.5 oz/100 g Serrano ham in one piece, finely diced
— 3.5 oz/100 g  Spanish chorizo, casings removed, finely diced
— 2 cups (250 g) canned, frozen, or fresh shelled peas, rinsed and drained
— salt
— 3.5 oz/100 g Parmesan cheese, grated, to serve

Put rice and 3 cups/710 ml water in a medium saucepan and bring to boil over medium-high heat. Cover and remove from heat.

Heat oil in a large frying pan over low heat. Add onion and pan-fry, stirring occasionally, for 8 minutes, or until it starts to brown. Add ham and chorizo and cook, stirring frequently, for 1 minute. Add rice, mixing it in well with a wooden spoon to ensure everything heats through evenly. Cook for about 5 minutes, then add peas, season with salt, and stir again.

Transfer rice to a warmed serving dish and serve the grated Parmesan separately.

# Rice with Bacon, Sausages, and Bonito

*Serves 8*
*Cook time: 15 minutes*

— 1 ½ cups (160 g) quick-cooking rice
— 2 tablespoons sunflower oil
— 4 frankfurters, quartered
— 2 thick slices (rashers) bacon, cut
  into strips
— 1 green bell pepper, finely chopped
— 1 large scallion (spring onion), finely
  chopped
— 2 stalks celery, thinly sliced
— scant ½ cup (2 oz/50 g) black olives,
  pitted and halved
— 2 (7 oz/200 g) cans oil-packed bonito
  or tuna, drained and flaked
— soy sauce

Put rice and 1½ cups/355 ml water in a pot with a tight-fitting lid and bring to a boil. Cover and remove from heat.

Heat oil in a large frying pan over medium-high heat. Add frankfurters and bacon and pan-fry, stirring occasionally, until cooked through. Add bell pepper and scallion, reduce heat to low, and cook, stirring frequently, until onion is softened but not colored.

Add rice to the pan and pan-fry it for a few minutes, then add celery, olives, and tuna. Season with soy sauce to taste, stir well, and serve hot.

# Rice with Jumbo Shrimp (King Prawns)

*Serves 6*
*Cook time: 20 minutes*

— ½ chicken stock cube
— generous 3 cups/750 ml boiling water, plus extra if needed
— ¾ cup (175 ml) olive oil
— 1 lb 2 oz (500 g) frozen peas
— 1 small onion, finely chopped
— 1 clove garlic, finely chopped
— 1¾ cups (215 g) quick-cooking rice
— 2 large tomatoes, peeled, seeded, and chopped
— pinch of saffron threads
— 2 tablespoons finely chopped parsley
— 2¼ lb (1 kg) jumbo shrimp (king prawns), unpeeled but rinsed
— salt

Dissolve stock cube in the boiling water

Heat 1 tablespoon of the oil over medium heat in a heavy-based pan. Add peas, cover, and let cook until tender, 3 minutes. Set aside and keep warm.

Meanwhile, heat the remaining oil in a paella pan or shallow heavy-based flameproof pan over low heat. Add onion and garlic and pan-fry, stirring occasionally, for 8 minutes, or until onions start to brown. Add rice and stir it around for a couple minutes until all the grains are coated.

Pour in the stock, tomatoes, saffron, parsley, shrimp, and peas. Stir well and season with salt. Bring to a boil, then reduce heat to low and cook, uncovered and without stirring, until rice is tender. The rice should not be dry, so add a little extra boiling water, if necessary.

# Rice with Swiss Chard and Navy (Haricot) Beans

*Serves 4–6*
*Cook time: 30 minutes*

— 3 tablespoons olive oil
— 1 onion, finely chopped
— 2 tablespoons tomato paste (puree)
— 1 clove garlic
— 1 sprig parsley, finely chopped
— 1 bay leaf
— ½ teaspoon paprika
— 2 (14 oz/395 g) cans navy (haricot) beans, rinsed, or 3 cups (540 g) cooked navy (haricot) beans
— 1 lb 2 oz (500 g) Swiss chard, rinsed and chopped
— salt
— 1½ cups (160 g) quick-cooking rice
— 1 (7 oz / 200 g) can cooked snails (optional)

Bring 8½ cups/2 L of water to a boil in a saucepan over medium-high heat.

Meanwhile, heat oil in a large frying pan with a tight-fitting lid over low heat. Add onion and pan-fry, stirring occasionally, for about 6 minutes, or until softened but not colored.

Add tomato paste (puree), garlic, parsley, and bay leaf and stir for about 3 minutes. Remove from heat and stir in paprika. Set aside.

Add beans, Swiss chard, and onion to the boiling water, season with salt, and cover. After 10 minutes, reserving the liquid, drain the chard. Return mixture to the pan. Stir in rice and generous 3 cups/750 ml of the liquid and season with salt. Bring liquid to a boil over medium-high heat, stirring occasionally. Partially cover and simmer for 10 minutes, or until rice is tender. Garnish with snails, if desired.

# Rice with Tomato, Sausage, Peas, and Bell Peppers

*Serves 6*
*Cook time: 25 minutes*

— 1 quantity Tomato Sauce
  (page 231)
— ⅔ cup/150 ml sunflower oil
— 1 large onion, finely chopped
— 1 clove garlic, peeled
— 1 sprig parsley
— salt
— 4 fresh sausages (350 g), halved across
— 2¾ cups (1 lb 5 oz/600 g) Calasparra
  or other short-grain rice
— 1 chicken stock cube, crumbled
— 6 cups/1.5 L boiling water
— 3.5 oz/100 g jarred roasted red
  peppers, drained
— ½ cup (75 g) canned or cooked frozen
  peas, drained and rinsed

Prepare tomato sauce in advance. Set aside.

Preheat the oven to 375°F/180°C/Gas Mark 4.

Heat oil in a paella pan or shallow heavy-based ovenproof pan over medium heat. Add onion and pan-fry, stirring occasionally, for 4 minutes, or until softened but not colored. Crush the garlic in a mortar with parsley and a little salt (to prevent the garlic slipping), then add it to the pan with the sausages and tomato sauce and let pan-fry a little. Next add rice and stir for 3 to 4 minutes.

Dissolve the stock cube in the boiling water. Pour into pan with bell peppers and season with salt, but take care as both the garlic and the stock cube will be salty. Let the liquid come to a boil, then cover the pan, put it in the oven and stir occasionally so that rice stays loose. Cook for 15 to 20 minutes, until rice is tender and all the liquid has been absorbed. Add peas toward the end of the cooking time. Remove from oven and let stand for 5 minutes before serving.

# Legumes

Beans and pulses are both proteins and fillers of hearty stews typical of the North and Central regions. These dishes came out of the impoverished countryside, where meat and fish were luxuries used sparingly and more as flavoring than the main event. Lentejas guisadas (lentils stewed with tomatoes, onions, and thickened with bread), and Fabada (white bean stew with chorizo and bacon), are some of the most satisfying comfort foods.

# White Beans with Sausages and Bacon

*Serves 6*
*Cook time: 30 minutes*

— 4½ cups (500 g) cooked white
  beans, such as lima (butter) beans
— 2 slices (rashers) bacon
— bouquet garni: 1 sprig fresh parsley,
  1 bay leaf, and 1 clove garlic tied
  together in muslin
— 6 frankfurters
— 3 tablespoons olive oil
— 6 fresh sausages (about 4 oz/
  115 g each)
— salt
— 3 tablespoons (45 g) butter
— 1 teaspoon chopped parsley

Put beans in a saucepan and pour in water to cover. Add bacon, bouquet garni, and frankfurters. Bring to a boil and simmer for 23 minutes.

Meanwhile, heat oil in a frying pan over medium heat. Add fresh sausages and cook, turning occasionally, until browned all over and cooked through. (Prick the sausages first if they have artificial casings.)

Season beans to taste with salt.

Remove and discard the bouquet garni. Melt butter in another saucepan and add parsley. Using a slotted spoon, transfer beans to the butter and parsley mixture and stir well.

Divide the beans among 6 warmed plates. Add a piece of ham, 2 pieces of bacon, a frankfurter, and a fried sausage to each and serve hot.

# Bean Stew

*Serves 6*
*Cook time: 30 minutes*

— 6 cups/1.4 L vegetable stock or water
— 1 large onion, cut into 4 pieces
— 2 cloves garlic, peeled
— 2 links Spanish chorizo (about
   5 oz/140 g each)
— 3½ oz/100 g bacon
— pinch of saffron threads
— 6 cups (2 lb 10 oz/1.2 kg) cooked
   beans
— salt

Pour stock into a saucepan, add onion and garlic and bring to a simmer over medium-low heat.

Meanwhile, sear the chorizo in a frying pan over high heat for about 3 minutes, making sure all the sides are evenly browned.

Transfer the chorizo to the simmering stock and simmer for 15 minutes.

While chorizo cooks, in the same frying pan over high heat, cook bacon, stirring constantly for about 5 minutes. Transfer bacon to the saucepan with stock and chorizo. Crush saffron in a mortar and stir in 2 tablespoons of the hot stock.

When stock has simmered for 15 minutes, remove onion and garlic and add beans and saffron mixture. Simmer until beans are warmed through, about 5 minutes. Season to taste with salt and serve.

Notes: This bean stew is much better made the previous day and reheated. It is also usual to remove a ladleful of beans, make a purée with them, and then use the purée to thicken the stew.

Legumes

# Lentil Stew

*Serves 6*
*Cook time: 30 minutes*

— generous 1 cup/275 ml olive oil
— 2 slices bread
— 1 small onion, finely diced
— 1 tomato, peeled, seeded, and chopped
— ½ teaspoon paprika
— 9 cups (1.8 kg) cooked lentils
— 1 clove garlic, peeled
— salt
— 1 sprig parsley
— 2–3 tablespoons vegetable stock
  or water

Heat oil in a large frying pan over medium heat. Add slices of bread and cook, turning occasionally, until crisp and evenly golden. Drain on paper towels and set aside.

Drain off most of the oil, leaving just enough to cover the base of the frying pan, and reheat. Add onion and cook over medium-low heat, stirring occasionally, for about 6 minutes, until beginning to brown. Add tomato and cook, stirring occasionally, for 8 minutes. Remove pan from the heat and stir in paprika.

Fold tomato mixture into lentils until combined.

Pound garlic in a mortar with a pinch of salt, parsley, and fried bread. Mix in the vegetable stock or water, then stir into the pan containing the lentils and tomatoes.

Season to taste with salt and cook for another 10 minutes; serve hot in a soup tureen.

# Lentils with Bacon and Sausages

*Serves 6*
*Cook time: 15 minutes*

— 12 small sausages (about 2 oz/
   50 g each)
— generous 1 cup/275 ml olive oil
— 9 oz/250 g slab bacon, cubed
— 9 cups (1.8 kg) cooked green
   Puy lentils, drained
— salt

Prick sausages if they have artificial casings.

Heat oil in a large frying pan over medium-high heat. Add the sausages and cook, turning frequently, for about 5 minutes, until lightly browned and cooked through. Remove from the pan and keep warm.

Drain off all but about half the oil from the frying pan and reheat. Add cubes of bacon and cook, stirring, for about 3 minutes. Add lentils, stir well, and season to taste with salt. Put lentils into a warm serving dish, place sausages on top and serve hot.

Note: Cook lentils in stock and if you would prefer a little more liquid in this finished dish, reserve some of the lentil cooking liquid and add it to achieve the desired consistency. It is worth reserving the cooking liquid anyway in case there are lentils left over. They can be pureed in a food processor to make a thick soup; garnish the soup with croutons or a little white rice.

Patatas y pasta

# Potatoes and Pasta

Potatoes are incredibly popular in Spain, and those
from Galicia have a particularly sweet flavor and waxy
texture. Arguably the post popular national potato dish
is patatas bravas, served drizzled with chile sauce
(use Yukon Gold potatoes, which result in patatas
with beautiful fluffy middles and crunchy outsides).
The Spanish serve potatoes in seemingly endless
permutations: baked in tomato sauce, with clams,
and with chorizo and bacon, among others. While
pasta is often associated with Italy, the Spanish love
to dress it with green pepper and ham for a quick and
comforting meal.

# Patatas Bravas

*Serves 4*
*Cook time: 20 minutes*

— 12 small potatoes, unpeeled, cut into
  wedges
— 2 tablespoons olive oil
— 1 tablespoon white wine vinegar
— 1 clove garlic, finely chopped
— 1 teaspoon chili powder or
  Worcestershire sauce
— pinch of hot paprika
— salt

Bring a large pan of salted water to a boil. Add potatoes and cook for 15 minutes, until tender but not falling apart. Drain and let cool, then peel and slice or dice. Transfer to a plate or tray.

Mix together the oil, vinegar, garlic, chili powder or Worcestershire sauce, and paprika in a bowl. Pour mixture over potatoes, season with salt, and serve hot.

# Potatoes with Clams

*Serves 4–6*
*Cook time: 30 minutes*

— 9 oz/250 g live clams in their shells,
 washed twice in salted water
— 6 tablespoons olive oil
— 1 small onion, finely chopped
— 2 tomatoes, peeled, seeded, and
 chopped
— 3¼ lb/1.5 kg potatoes, parboiled,
 peeled, and cut into large pieces
— 1 tablespoon all-purpose (plain) flour
— 1 clove garlic, peeled
— salt
— 1 sprig parsley
— pinch of saffron threads

Discard any clams with broken shells or any that do not shut when sharply tapped.

Put clams in a saucepan, with ¼ cup/50 ml water, and a pinch of salt. Cover and cook over high heat for 3–5 minutes, until clams open. Remove from heat and lift out clams with a slotted spoon. Discard any that remain shut. Strain liquid into a bowl through a sieve lined with cheesecloth (muslin) and reserve. Remove clams from their shells and add to the bowl.

Meanwhile, heat oil in a small frying pan over medium heat. Add onion and cook, stirring, for 3 minutes. Add tomatoes and cook, stirring, for 5 minutes. Transfer mixture to a larger saucepan set over low heat. Stir in potatoes and flour. Pound garlic in a mortar with a pinch of salt, parsley, and saffron. Stir in 2–3 tablespoons of reserved liquid, and add to the potatoes.

Add clams with liquid and enough water just to cover potatoes. Bring to a boil, then simmer for about 15 minutes, until potatoes are tender. Serve hot.

# Potatoes Baked in Tomato Sauce

*Serves 6*
*Cook time: 30 minutes*

— Tomato Sauce (page 231)
— generous 2 cups/500 ml sunflower oil
— 3¼ lb/1.5 kg potatoes, thinly sliced
— 5 oz/150 g bacon, diced
— salt
— ½ cup (2 oz/60 g) grated cheese, such as Cheddar or Gruyère
— 2 tablespoons (30 grams) butter

Preheat the oven to 450°F/230°C/Gas Mark 8.

Bring tomato sauce to a simmer in a saucepan.

Meanwhile, heat oil in a large frying pan over medium-high heat. Working in batches, add the potato slices and cook until light golden brown. Remove with a slotted spoon and drain on paper towels.

Add bacon to the pan and cook until lightly browned, then drain well and set aside.

Layer potato slices, bacon, and tomato sauce in a deep ovenproof baking dish, seasoning each layer with salt. Sprinkle cheese on top and dot with butter. Bake for about 15 minutes, uncover, and continue to bake until golden and bubbling. Serve hot, straight from the dish.

# Potatoes with Chorizo and Bacon

*Serves 4*
*Cook time: 30 minutes*

— 3 tablespoons lard
— 5 tablespoons sunflower oil
— 2 oz/50 g Spanish chorizo, peeled and thinly sliced
— 3.5 oz/100 g bacon, cut into ½-inch/1 cm-wide strips
— 3¼ lb/1.5 kg cooked potatoes
— salt
— 1 tablespoon chopped parsley
— 1 clove garlic, finely chopped

Melt lard with oil in a saucepan or large frying pan over medium high heat. (It needs to be big enough to hold the potatoes in a single layer.) Add chorizo and bacon and cook over medium heat, stirring constantly, for a few minutes. Add potatoes, season with salt, and cook over low heat, shaking the pan occasionally, for 25 minutes, or until the potatoes are evenly browned.

Just before serving, sprinkle with parsley and garlic and stir for a few minutes more. Transfer to a warm serving dish and serve hot.

Note: Some types of chorizo become hard with prolonged cooking. To prevent this, cook the slices with the bacon, then remove and set aside. About 10 minutes before serving, return the slices of chorizo to the pan.

# Pasta with Peppers and Ham

*Serves 4*
*Cook time: 20 minutes*

— 3 tablespoons olive oil
— 3 red onions, sliced
— 2 large jarred roasted red peppers, cut into strips
— 7 oz/200 g thinly sliced Serrano ham, cut into strips
— 2 tablespoons capers, rinsed and drained
— 4 tablespoons chopped fresh basil
— salt and pepper
— 1 lb/455 g tagliatelle

Heat oil in a large frying pan over low heat. Add onions and cook, stirring occasionally, for about 5 minutes, or until softened and translucent. Remove pan from heat, stir in pepper strips, ham, capers, and basil. Season with salt and pepper and transfer to a bowl.

Meanwhile, bring a large saucepan of salted water to a boil. Add tagliatelle, bring back to a boil, and cook for 8 to 10 minutes, until al dente. Drain well.

Toss pasta with the mixture in the bowl. Serve warm or cold.

Note: for a contrast of textures, cook ham in a frying pan until crisp before adding to the recipe.

# Vegetables and Mushrooms

In the forests and mountains around Spain, from the Sierra Nevada in the South to the great Irati forest of Navarra, to the rolling green hills of Catalonia and the Basque Country, wild mushrooms are considered gold. Their whereabouts are a closely guarded secret by foragers. In the fall, mushrooms become a superstar ingredient, appearing in such dishes as hearty Wild Mushroom and Anchovy Fricassee. Other vegetables shine, too: leeks are tucked into flan; pumpkin is cubed and fried; asparagus is tossed with garlic, vinegar, and paprika; and tomatoes are stretched beyond their expected role—reinvented in a refreshing and palate-cleansing sorbet.

# Leek Flan

*Serves 6*
*Cook time: 25 minutes*

— butter, for greasing
— 4 leeks, trimmed and cut into ¾-inch/
2 cm slices
— 3 eggs
— generous 2 cups/500 ml milk, at room
temperature
— 2 teaspoons cornstarch (cornflour)
— salt and pepper
— 5 oz/150 g cooked ham, finely chopped
— 1⅓ cups (5 oz/150 g) grated Gruyère
cheese

Preheat the oven to 400°F/200°C/Gas Mark 6. Generously grease a (8-inch/20 cm) square baking dish.

Bring a saucepan of salted water to a boil over medium-high heat. Add leeks and cook for 15 minutes, or until very tender. Drain leeks well.

Meanwhile, beat together the eggs and milk in a bowl. Add a small amount of this mixture to the cornstarch (cornflour) to make a paste, then add the cornstarch mixture to the milk mixture and season with salt and pepper.

Stir leeks, ham, and cheese into the egg mixture, then pour mixture into the prepared dish. Bake for 20 minutes, or until set. Cut into slices and serve hot or cold.

# Fried Artichokes

*Serves 6*
*Cook time: 10 minutes*

— 2–4 tablespoons olive oil
— 2 tablespoons (1 oz/25 g) lard (optional)
— 14 oz/385 g canned or thawed frozen
  artichoke hearts
— 5 oz/150 g Serrano ham, diced
— 1 tablespoon chopped parsley
— salt

Add 2 tablespoons of the oil and lard, if using, to a frying pan. If not using lard, add 2 tablespoons more oil. Heat over medium heat. Add artichokes and ham and cook gently, stirring occasionally, for 7 minutes. Sprinkle with parsley, season with salt, and serve hot.

# Fried Pumpkin

*Serves 4*
*Cook time: 20 minutes*

— 4 leeks, cut into 1-inch/2.5 cm lengths
 and rinsed well
— 3¼ lb/1.5 kg pumpkin, peeled and
 cubed
— 1 cup/250 ml olive oil
— 3–4 slices bread, crusts removed,
 cubed
— 3 cloves garlic, lightly crushed
— salt

Bring a pan of salted water to a boil over high heat. Add leeks and cook for 5 minutes. Add pumpkin and cook for about 7 minutes, until pumpkin is fork-tender. Drain off the water, cover the pan, and set aside.

Heat oil in a large frying pan over medium heat. Add bread and cook, stirring frequently, until evenly browned. Remove with a slotted spoon and drain on paper towels.

Pour most of the oil out of the pan, leaving just enough to cover the base. Return the pan to the heat, add garlic, and cook for a few minutes until well browned. Remove and discard garlic. Add pumpkin, leeks, and croutons to the pan and cook over low heat for 5 minutes. Season to taste with salt, and serve hot.

Champiñones rellenos

# Stuffed Mushrooms

*Serves 4*
*Cook time: 25 minutes*

— 4 large portobello mushrooms,
   wiped clean
— 2 tablespoons olive oil
— 2 shallots, chopped
— salt
— juice of ½ lemon, strained

Preheat the oven to 350°F/180°C/Gas Mark 4.

Pull stems out of mushroom caps and
chop the stems.

Heat oil in a small frying pan over low heat. Add
the mushroom stems and shallots and cook,
stirring occasionally, for about 5 minutes. Season
with salt, stir in a few drops of the lemon juice
and cook for another 5–8 minutes, until nicely
browned.

Put mushroom caps on a baking sheet and divide
filling among them, then bake for 5 minutes.
Increase the oven temperature to 425°F/220°C/
Gas Mark 7 and bake, shaking the pan
occasionally, for another 5 minutes.

Fricasé de setas con anchoas

# Wild Mushroom and Anchovy Fricassee

*Serves 4*
*Cook time: 30 minutes*

— 4 tablespoons olive oil
— 2¼ lb/1 kg porcini (cèpes) or other wild mushrooms, cleaned and cut into large pieces
— 12 oil-packed anchovy fillets, drained
— 2 cloves garlic, peeled
— 1 cup (250 ml) vegetable stock, homemade or purchased
— pepper
— 1 tablespoon chopped parsley

Heat oil in a flameproof earthenware casserole or a large frying pan over high heat. Add mushrooms and pan-fry, stirring frequently, for 5 minutes.

Meanwhile, put anchovies and garlic in a large mortar and crush them to a paste. Bring stock to a simmer in a small pot.

Stir stock and contents of the mortar into mushrooms and season with pepper. Cover the pan and let simmer over low heat for 15 minutes. Sprinkle parsley into the pan, cover, and simmer for another 5 minutes. Serve hot, either in a serving dish or on small plates.

# Fried Green Asparagus with Garlic, Vinegar, and Paprika

*Serves 6*
Cook time; 30 minutes

— 6 tablespoons olive oil
— 3 slices bread, crusts removed
— 2 cloves garlic, peeled
— 4½ lb/2 kg asparagus, trimmed and cut into 1½-inch/4 cm lengths
— ½ teaspoon paprika
— 3 tablespoons white wine vinegar
— salt
— 1 teaspoon chopped parsley

Heat oil in a frying pan over medium heat. Add bread and cook, turning occasionally, for a few minutes, until golden brown on both sides. Remove from pan and set aside.

Add garlic to the pan and cook, stirring frequently, for a few minutes, until golden brown. Transfer garlic to a mortar, add fried bread, and pound with a pestle. Set aside.

Pour oil from the frying pan into a saucepan and heat it. Add asparagus and pan-fry for 2–3 minutes. Remove pan from heat and stir in paprika, then pour in 2 cups/450 ml hot water. Return pan to medium-high heat, cover, and cook, shaking the pan occasionally, for 12–15 minutes, until the asparagus is just tender.

Add vinegar and a little of the asparagus cooking liquid to the mixture in the mortar and stir well, then stir back into the saucepan. Season with a little salt and cook for another 5 minutes. Sprinkle with parsley and serve hot.

Pisto de calabacín

# Zucchini Ratatouille

*Serves 6*
*Cook time: 25 minutes*

— 3–5 tablespoons olive oil
— 1 cup (250 g) chopped onions
— 4 ½ lb/2 kg zucchini (courgettes), diced
— Basic Tomato Sauce (page 231)
— 1 teaspoon sugar
— 2 green bell peppers, diced (optional)
— salt

Heat 3 tablespoons of the oil in a saucepan. Add onions and cook over medium heat, stirring frequently, for about 2 minutes, or until softened and translucent. Increase the heat to high, add zucchini, and cook, stirring occasionally, for another 4 minutes, until lightly browned.

Meanwhile, in a saucepan, bring tomato sauce to a boil; season with sugar.

Pour tomato sauce over hot zucchini. Reduce heat to medium, cover, and stir occasionally for 10 minutes, adding a little water if the mixture is becoming too thick.

If using green peppers, heat 2 tablespoons oil in a small frying pan over medium heat. Add peppers, cover, and cook, stirring occasionally, for about 15 minutes. Stir the peppers into the zucchini just before serving.

Serve in a warm deep dish.

Vegetables and Mushrooms

# Coated Green Beans

*Serves 4*
*Cook time: 30 minutes*

— 1¼ lb/570 g young green beans
— 2¾ cups/500 ml sunflower oil
— 1–2 eggs
— ½ cup (60 g) all-purpose (plain) flour
— 2 slices Fried Bread (see page 231)
— 1 large clove garlic
— 3–4 sprigs parsley
— 3 tablespoons white wine vinegar
— salt

Bring a pot of salted water to a boil. Add beans and cook for about 8 minutes, or until tender. Drain well and pat dry.

Meanwhile, heat oil in a deep-fryer or deep saucepan to 350°–375°F/180°–190°C, or until a cube of day-old bread browns in 30 seconds.

Beat eggs in a shallow dish and spread out flour in another shallow dish. One at a time, dredge beans first in flour and then dip in egg. Add them to the hot oil, in batches, and cook until golden. Drain well and put into a deep serving dish. Reserve the frying oil.

Pound fried bread, garlic, and parsley in a mortar and stir in vinegar and 1 cup plus 2 tablespoons/275 ml of the reserved frying oil. Mix well, pour over beans, and let stand for 15 minutes before serving.

# Stuffed Beets

*Serves 4*
*Cook time: 10 minutes*

— 4 cooked beets
— 2 eggs, hard-boiled (see page 230), peeled and halved
— Scant ½ cup (3.5 oz/100 g) long-grain rice, cooked
— 1 apple, peeled and diced
— ½ small onion, finely chopped
— 1 tablespoon chopped parsley
— 1 tablespoon red wine vinegar
— 3 tablespoons olive oil
— salt and pepper

Peel beets and cut a slice like a little hat off the top of each one. Hollow out the centers, taking care not to break the "shells." Dice the scooped-out flesh and put in a bowl.

Scoop the yolks out of hard-boiled eggs and set aside. Finely chop the egg whites and add to the diced beets along with rice, apple, onion, and parsley.

Whisk together vinegar and oil in another bowl, stir in egg yolks, and season with salt and pepper, then pour over beet and rice mixture. Season to taste with salt and pepper and use to fill beet shells. Refrigerate until ready to serve.

# Tomatoes Filled with Sardines, Green Peppers, and Olives

*Serves 6*
*Cook time: 20 minutes*

*For the vinaigrette*
— 3 tablespoons sunflower oil
— 1 tablespoon white wine vinegar
— ½ teaspoon mustard
— 1 teaspoon chopped parsley
— salt

*For the stuffed tomatoes*
— 3 tablespoons olive oil
— 2 green bell peppers, diced
— salt
— 9 large oil-packed canned sardines (8 oz/225 g), drained
— 12 tomatoes, seeded, salted, and drained
— ½ cup (3.5 oz/100 g) pimiento-stuffed olives, halved
— lettuce leaves

Whisk the vinaigrette ingredients together.

To make stuffed tomatoes, heat oil in a large frying pan over low heat. Add green peppers, cover, and cook, shaking the pan occasionally, for 10 minutes, until softened. Just before the end of cooking, lightly season with salt.

Remove the skin and bones from sardines and flake the flesh into a bowl with a fork. Add sautéed peppers and vinaigrette, mix well, and divide mixture among the tomatoes. Refrigerate for 2 hours before serving. Top with olives, garnish with the lettuce leaves, and serve.

# Tomato Sorbet

*Serves 4–6*
*Cook time: 30 minutes (plus freezing time)*

— 3¼ lb/1.5 kg very ripe tomatoes,
   peeled, seeded, and chopped
— 1 small onion, chopped
— 1 sprig mint
— 1 sprig basil
— 1 sprig marjoram
— 1 tablespoon tomato paste (purée)
— juice of 2 lemons
— 2 tablespoons light brown sugar
— lemon slices (optional)

Put tomato, onion, mint, basil, marjoram, and ¾ cup/175 ml water in a saucepan. Bring to a boil over high and cook, stirring constantly, until water is completely evaporated, about 10 minutes. Reduce heat and simmer for about 15 minutes. Transfer mixture to a food processor and process until smooth.

Stir in tomato paste, lemon juice, and brown sugar and leave to cool. Freeze for at least 4 hours. Just before serving, remove sorbet from the freezer, beat gently to break the ice and serve in glasses, garnished with slices of lemon, if using. Serve sorbet at the beginning of a meal.

Pisto manchego

# Manchegan Ratatouille

*Serves 10*
*Cook time: 25 minutes*

— ½ cup plus 2 tablespoons/150 ml olive
  oil
— 1½ cups (7 oz/200 g) diced Spanish
  chorizo
— 1½ cups (7 oz/200 g) diced ham
— 2¼ lb/1 kg onions, chopped
— 2¼ lb/1 kg green bell peppers, diced
— 2¼ lb/1 kg zucchini (courgettes), diced
— 2¼ lb/1 kg tomatoes, peeled and
  chopped
— salt
— croutons

Heat oil in a saucepan over high heat. Add chorizo and ham and cook, stirring occasionally, for 3 minutes. Remove with a slotted spoon and set aside.

Add onions and green peppers to the pan and cook, stirring frequently, for 6 minutes, until softened. Add zucchini and tomatoes, mix well, cover, and simmer gently for 10 minutes, until cooked through and soft. Season to taste with salt, add chorizo and ham, and heat through for a few minutes. Serve hot with croutons.

Champiñones al ajillo

# Garlic Mushrooms

*Serves 6*
*Cook time: 15 minutes*

— ½ cup plus 1 tablespoon/135 ml
sunflower oil
— 3¼ lb/1.5 kg button mushrooms
— salt
— 3 cloves garlic, chopped
— 2 tablespoons chopped parsley

Preheat the oven to 350°F/180°C/Gas Mark 4.

Divide oil and mushrooms among 6 ovenproof earthenware ramekins or other individual cooking dishes. (If you don't have individual dishes, just cook the ingredients all together in a frying pan and divide among 6 serving dishes or ramekins when you are done.) Add some salt and garlic to each.

Arrange ramekins on a baking sheet and bake for 5 minutes. Increase the oven temperature to 425°F/220°C/Gas Mark 7 and bake, shaking the dishes occasionally, for another 10 minutes. Sprinkle parsley over mushrooms and serve hot.

# Eggs

In the Boqueria market in Barcelona, there is an entire stall devoted to eggs, but the most prized are those from Calafell, a small town in the hinterland where the yolks are a bit sweeter and yellower than anywhere else. Eggs in Spain are stars of their own show, in the form of a classic Spanish tortilla, or *revueltos* (scrambled) with spinach and shrimp. Poached, hard-boiled, or coddled, you are as likely to find eggs in Spain served for dinner as for breakfast.

# Coddled Eggs on Toast with Spinach

*Serves 4*
*Cook time: 20 minutes*

— 4 thick slices bread
— 1 lb 2 oz/500 g spinach, coarse stems trimmed
— 2 tablespoons (30 g) butter
— 7 tablespoons (100 ml) half-and half (single cream)
— 4 eggs
— 3.5 oz/100 g cooked ham, chopped
— 2 tablespoons grated Gruyère cheese
— salt and pepper

Preheat broiler (grill) to high. Toast bread for 2 minutes on each side, until golden but still soft. Do not turn off broiler.

Bring a large pan of salted water to a boil. Blanch spinach for 1 minute, drain, and press out all liquid.

Melt butter in a frying pan over low heat. Cook spinach for a few minutes; remove from heat and stir in cream. Keep spinach and toast warm.

Bring a pan of water with 2 tablespoons salt to a boil. Put eggs into a wire basket and place in the water. When water returns to a boil, cook eggs for exactly 5 minutes, then remove from heat. Run cold water over eggs until completely cold.

Carefully peel eggs. Arrange toasts on a baking sheet. Spread half of spinach mixture over toast and sprinkle each with ham. Carefully place an egg over each toast; top with remaining spinach mixture and cheese. Broil until cheese melts but doesn't brown. Season with salt and pepper and serve hot.

# Scrambled Eggs with Spinach and Shrimp (Prawns)

*Serves 6*
*Cook time: 20 minutes*

— 2¼ lb/1 kg spinach, coarse stems
 trimmed
— salt
— 3½ tablespoons (1.75 oz/50 g) butter or
 5 tablespoons olive oil
— 12 oz/340 g shrimp (prawns), peeled
— Fried Bread (page 231; optional)
— 8 eggs, lightly beaten

Wash spinach in several changes of water, drain slightly, then put into a pan with just the water clinging to its leaves. Add a pinch of salt and cook over medium heat, stirring occasionally, for 8–10 minutes, until wilted. Drain well, pressing out as much liquid as possible with the back of a spoon. Chop it finely.

Heat butter or oil in a frying pan over medium heat. Add shrimp and cook, stirring occasionally, for 2 minutes. Stir in spinach and cook, stirring constantly, for 3 minutes, until shrimp are cooked through.

Meanwhile, if desired, make the fried bread.

Season eggs with salt, pour into the frying pan with shrimp and spinach and cook, stirring frequently, for a few minutes, until eggs begin to set. Put into a warm serving dish and serve hot, garnished with fried bread, if desired.

Tortilla de patatas a la española

# Spanish Tortilla

*Serves 6*
*Cook time: 20 minutes*

— generous 2 cups (500 ml) plus
  2 tablespoons olive oil
— 2¼ lb/1 kg potatoes, halved lengthwise
  and thinly sliced crosswise
— salt
— 8 eggs
— Mayonnaise, homemade (page 230) or
  purchased, to serve (optional)

Heat 2 cups olive oil in an 11-inch (28 cm) frying pan over medium heat. Add potato slices and cook, stirring occasionally, until softened and lightly browned. Season with salt, remove from the frying pan and drain well.

Beat eggs vigorously with a pinch of salt in a large bowl for 1 minute. Add potato slices and stir with a fork. Heat the remaining 2 tablespoons olive oil in the frying pan over high heat. Tip in egg mixture and cook, gently shaking the frying pan occasionally, until the underside is set and lightly browned.

Invert tortilla onto the lid of a pan or a plate, then gently slide it back into the frying pan, cooked side up. Cook, shaking the pan occasionally, until the underside is set and golden brown. Serve hot, cut into wedges. If desired, spread mayonnaise on top or serve it on the side.

# Vegetable Tortilla

*Serves 4*
*Cook time: 30 minutes*

— 4 tablespoons olive oil
— 1 small onion, chopped
— 1 green bell pepper, finely chopped
— 1 red bell pepper, finely chopped
— 1 small eggplant (aubergine), diced
— 1 small zucchini (courgette), diced
— 2 tomatoes, peeled, seeded, and diced
— 8 eggs
— salt

Heat oil in an 11-inch (28 cm) frying pan over medium-high heat. Add onion and pan-fry, stirring occasionally, for 2 minutes. Stir in bell peppers, eggplant, and zucchini and cook for 8 minutes, or until browned. Add tomatoes and cook for about 10 minutes, or until the liquid has evaporated and the mixture has thickened, about 10 minutes.

Beat eggs vigorously with a pinch of salt in a large bowl. Tip in the egg mixture and cook, partially covered, gently shaking the pan occasionally, until the underside is set and lightly browned, about 3 minutes. Invert tortilla onto a lid of a pan or a plate, then gently slide it back into the frying pan, cooked side up. Cook, gently shaking the frying pan occasionally, until the underside is set and golden brown, about 3 minutes. Serve hot or at room temperature, cut into wedges.

Note: If you have any of this left over, it is delicious served cold with a little mayonnaise spread across the top.

# Hard-Boiled Eggs au Gratin

*Serves 6*
*Cook time: 30 minutes*

— 1⅓ cups (9 oz/250 g) diced
  mushrooms
— juice of ½ lemon
— 5 tablespoons butter, plus more
  as needed
— 4 tablespoons sunflower oil
— 1 onion, finely chopped
— 2 tablespoons all-purpose (plain) flour
— 2¼ cups/500 ml milk
— salt
— 9 eggs, hard-boiled (see page 230),
  peeled, and halved lengthwise
— pinch of freshly grated nutmeg
— 3 tablespoons breadcrumbs

Put mushrooms, lemon juice, and 1½ tablespoons butter in a saucepan, cover, and cook over medium heat for 4 minutes until mushrooms begin to brown. Scrape into a bowl.

Meanwhile, heat 2 tablespoons of oil in a frying pan over medium heat. Add onion and cook, stirring occasionally, for about 6 minutes, or until beginning to brown. Add to mushrooms.

Meanwhile, melt 2 tablespoons butter with the remaining oil in a saucepan over medium heat. Stir in flour and cook, stirring constantly, for 2 minutes. Gradually stir in milk. Season with salt and cook, stirring constantly, for 6–8 minutes.

Spoon out 2 tablespoons of the sauce and add to mushroom mixture. Add egg yolks, nutmeg, and stir to combine. Fill egg white halves with this mixture, place in an ovenproof dish, and top with remaining sauce. Sprinkle with breadcrumbs, dot with remaining butter and bake for 10–15 minutes, until golden brown. Serve hot.

# Poached Eggs with Asparagus

*Serves 6*
*Cook time: 25 minutes*

— 18 spears asparagus, trimmed
— 4 tablespoons (60 g) butter
— 8 eggs
— 2 cups/475 ml milk
— 6 slices bread
— 2 tablespoons sunflower oil
— 2 tablespoons all-purpose (plain) flour
— salt
— pinch of freshly grated nutmeg
— 2 tablespoons white wine vinegar

Bring a large saucepan of salted water to a boil. Blanch asparagus for 3 minutes, or until bright green and slightly tender. Drain and set aside.

Melt 2 tablespoons butter in a frying pan over medium heat. Lightly beat 2 eggs in a shallow dish; pour milk into another shallow dish. Dip bread in milk, then in beaten eggs. (Reserve remaining milk.) Cook bread in the pan, in batches, until golden brown on both sides, about 90 seconds per side. Remove to a plate and keep warm.

Melt remaining butter in the oil in a separate frying pan over medium-low heat. Stir in flour and cook, stirring, for 2 minutes. Gradually stir in reserved milk. Cook, stirring, for 6–8 minutes, until thickened. Season with salt and nutmeg, and keep warm.

Poach remaining eggs, 3 at a time, in the gently simmering water with vinegar, for 4 minutes. Transfer bread to a warm serving dish and top with an egg on each slice, some, sauce, and asparagus.

# Shirred Eggs with Chicken Livers

*Serves 6*
*Cook time: 20 minutes*

— 3 tablespoons olive oil
— 1 small onion, finely chopped
— 6 small chicken livers, trimmed and
  cut into 4 pieces each
— 1 tablespoon potato starch (flour)
— 2 tablespoons sherry
— salt
— 4 tablespoons (60 g) butter
— 6 eggs
— 1 tablespoon chopped parsley

Preheat the oven to 325°F/160°C/Gas Mark 3.

Heat oil in a small frying pan over low heat. Add the onion and cook, stirring occasionally, for 5 minutes, or until softened and translucent. Add chicken livers and cook, stirring frequently, for 3 minutes. With a slotted spoon, remove livers and onions to a plate and set aside.

Stir potato flour in the frying pan and cook, stirring constantly, for 2 minutes. Gradually stir in sherry, a little at a time, then stir in 1 cup plus 2 tablespoons/275 ml water. Cook, stirring constantly, for 2–3 minutes, then return livers and onion to the pan and season with salt. Remove from heat and keep warm.

Divide butter among 6 egg dishes and melt in the oven. Break an egg into each dish and bake until the whites are opaque and the yolk seems just set, 8-10 minutes.

Gently reheat the sauce and spoon it over egg whites. Sprinkle with parsley and serve hot.

# Scrambled Eggs with Rice and Shrimp (Prawns)

*Serves 6*
*Cook time: 25 minutes*

— pinch of saffron threads, crushed
— 2 cups (14 oz/400 g) long-grain rice
— 9 oz/250 g shrimp (prawns), peeled
— 9 tablespoons (130 g) butter
— salt
— 12 eggs
— 6 tablespoons milk
— 4 tablespoons light (single) cream

Bring 3 quarts/3 L water to a boil in a saucepan. Add saffron to the pan; add rice and cook over high heat for about 15 minutes or until tender. Drain, run under cold running water, and drain again. Meanwhile, put shrimp, 1½ tablespoons butter, and a pinch of salt in a small saucepan. Cover and cook for 5 minutes, until shrimp are pink and cooked through.

Melt 4 tablespoons butter in a large frying pan. Add rice, season with salt, and heat through.

Beat eggs in another saucepan. Add shrimp, milk, remaining butter, and a pinch of salt. Put saucepan in a roasting pan, add hot water to come halfway up the saucepan, and whisk constantly, especially around the sides of the pan where eggs will set first. When mixture is thick and creamy, remove pan from heat as eggs will continue to cook off heat. Stir in cream.

Spoon rice into a ring mold and flip onto a warm serving plate. Put scrambled eggs and shrimp in the middle and serve hot.

Eggs

# Savory Custard

*Serves 6*
*Cook time: 30 minutes*

— butter, for greasing
— 8 eggs
— 3.5 oz/100 g Serrano ham, finely chopped
— 5 tablespoons sherry
— pinch of freshly grated nutmeg
— salt
— 3¼ cups (750 ml) warm milk

*For the tomato béchamel sauce*
— 1½ tablespoons (22 g) butter
— 2 tablespoons sunflower oil
— 1 tablespoon all-purpose (plain) flour
— 1 cup plus 2 tablespoons/275 ml milk
— 1 tablespoon tomato paste (purée) or 2 tablespoons Tomato Sauce (page 231)
— salt

Preheat the oven to 375°F/190°C/Gas Mark 5. Grease a 10-inch (25 cm) ring mold with butter.

Beat eggs in a bowl. Add ham, sherry, and nutmeg and season with salt (bearing in mind that ham is salty). Mix well, then gradually stir in milk, a little at a time. Pour mixture into the prepared pan (mold) and bake for 30 minutes, or until set and golden.

Meanwhile, make tomato béchamel sauce: Melt butter with oil in a pan and stir in flour. Gradually stir in milk, a little at a time, and bring to a biol, stirring constantly until thickened, 8–10 minutes. Stir in tomato paste or tomato sauce. Keep the sauce warm.

Remove custard from the oven and turn out on to a serving dish. Fill its center with béchamel sauce and serve hot.

# Fish and Shellfish

If you had to pinpoint the glittering jewels in Spain's
culinary crown, they would be fish and seafood.
Surrounded by the Mediterranean and Cantabrian seas
and the Atlantic Ocean, the supply ranges from meaty
turbot and silvery sardines to blue-shelled lobster,
river trout, and briny oysters, resulting in dishes like
Navarra-style trout, salt cod stewed in garlic, and crispy
fried squid. With a focus on simplicity, Spanish seafood
dishes underscore that pristine ingredients need very
little to truly shine.

# Crumb-Coated Cod with Tomato Sauce

*Serves 6*
*Cook time: 25 minutes*

— 1½ lb/750 g cod, cleaned and
    boned with heads removed, then
    washed and dried
— salt
— 1 egg
— ¾ cup (95 g) all-purpose (plain) flour
— 2 tablespoons sunflower oil
— lemon wedges, to serve
— sprigs parsley, to garnish (optional)
— Basic Tomato Sauce (page 231) or
    purchased, warm

Open up cod, season the insides with salt, and leave open.

Beat egg in a shallow dish and spread out flour in another. Heat oil in a frying pan. Working in batches, dip the fish first in the flour, shaking off any excess, and then in the beaten egg. Add to the hot oil and pan-fry for about 10 minutes, or until golden brown and the flesh flakes easily. Remove with a slotted spatula (fish slice), drain on paper towels, and keep warm while you pan-fry the remainder. Serve in a warmed serving dish with lemon wedges and garnished with sprigs of parsley, if desired. Serve tomato sauce hot in a sauceboat.

# Simple Fried Squid

*Serves 6*
*Cook time: 30 minutes*

— sunflower oil, for deep-frying
— 1¼ lb (565 g) cleaned squid, bodies
    cut crosswise into ½-inch (1 cm) rings
— salt
— 1 cup (125 g) all-purpose (plain) flour
— lemon wedges, to serve

Heat oil in a deep-fryer or deep saucepan to 350°–375°F/180°–190°C), or until a cube of day-old bread browns in 30 seconds.

Lightly season squid rings with salt and coat them in flour, shaking off any excess. Working in batches, add squid rings to the hot oil and cook until golden brown. Remove with a slotted spoon, drain well and keep warm while cooking the remaining batches.

Serve squid with lemon wedges on the side.

Note: Breadcrumbs can also be added to the flour.

# Crayfish in Wine and Tomato Sauce

*Serves 6*
*Cook time: 30 minutes*

— 3 tablespoons olive oil
— 2 large carrots, very finely chopped
— 1 small onion, very finely chopped
— 1 shallot, very finely chopped
— 2 very ripe tomatoes, seeded and chopped
— 1½ pounds/680 g large crayfish (about 36) or shrimp/prawns (about 48)
— 1 cup (250 ml) dry white wine
— 3 tablespoons brandy
— pinch of mixed dried herbs or 1 bouquet garni (see page 86)
— pinch of cayenne pepper
— 2 tablespoons (30 g) butter
— 1 tablespoon chopped parsley
— salt and pepper

Heat oil in a saucepan over low heat. Add carrots, onion, and shallot, cover, and cook for 5 minutes. Add 1 cup/250 ml water and tomatoes, cover, and cook for 10 minutes, until thickens into a sauce. Meanwhile, wash crayfish, in plenty of cold water. Remove intestines and set aside.

Put crayfish in a frying pan with wine, a pinch of salt, cover, and cook over high heat until red, 5 minutes. Warm brandy in a small pan for a few seconds, carefully ignite it (stand back), and pour over crayfish, stirring until the flames die down. Remove from heat and set aside.

Add crayfish mixture and herbs to tomatoes. Season with black pepper and cook for about 5 minutes. With a slotted spoon, transfer crayfish to a bowl and keep warm. Cook sauce for another 5 minutes; strain into a clean pan, pressing down hard and adding a little hot water if necessary. Add cayenne pepper, season to taste with salt, and add butter and crayfish. Sprinkle with parsley and cook for a few minutes more to heat through. Serve hot.

# Andalusian Fried Fish

*Serves 4*
*Cook time: 25 minutes*

— 2½ lb/1.1 kg fish fillets, such as small red mullet, sole, cod, or fresh anchovies
— sunflower oil, for deep-frying
— 2¼ cups (250 g) all-purpose (plain) flour
— salt
— lemon wedges, to serve

Rinse fish under cold running water and pat dry.

Heat oil in a deep-fryer or deep saucepan to 350°F/180°C, or until a cube of day-old bread browns in 30 seconds.

Spread flour out in a shallow dish. When the oil is hot, season fish with salt, then coat in flour, shaking off any excess. Working in batches, carefully add fish to the hot oil and cook until golden brown. Remove with a slotted spatula (fish slice), drain well, transfer to a serving dish, and either garnish with lemon wedges and serve at once while you cook the remaining batches, or keep warm until all the fish are cooked.

Note: These fried fish can be served as a tapa or as a main dish for a light lunch or supper. It is also good accompanied with garlic-flavored mayonnaise.

# Shrimp (Prawns) in Brick Pastry

*Makes 24*
*Cook time: 30 minutes*

— 2 tablespoons (30 g) butter, plus extra
  melted butter to brush pastry
— 1 large leek, trimmed and chopped
— 5 oz/150 g soft cream cheese
— salt and pepper
— 8 sheets brick or phyllo (filo) pastry,
  thawed if frozen
— 24 large shrimp/prawns (about
  ¾ lb/340 g), peeled and deveined

Preheat the oven to 400°F/200°C/Gas Mark 6.

Melt tablespoons butter in a saucepan over medium-high heat. Add leek and gently pan-fry until wilted and tender, about 5 minutes. Add cheese and stir until a creamy consistency forms. Season with salt and pepper, then remove pan from heat.

Cut pastry into 24 pieces. Put a little of the leek mixture and a shrimp onto each one, then fold the pastry to enclose the filling. Dampen the edges of the pastry with a little water and press down to seal. It is important that they are well sealed so the filling does not leak while being baked. Put pastries on a baking sheet and brush with melted butter. Bake for 15 minutes, or until golden brown and crisp. Let cool slightly, then serve.

# Mussels with Garlic and Parsley Butter

*Serves 6*
*Cook time: 15 minutes*

— 4½ lb/2 kg large mussels, scrubbed
  and debearded
— ¾ cup/175 ml white wine
— 1 shallot, chopped
— pinch of mixed dried herbs
— salt

*For the garlic and parsley butter*
— 2 sticks plus 2 tablespoons (9 oz/
  250 g) butter, at room temperature
— 2 cloves garlic, very finely chopped
— 3 tablespoons chopped parsley

Preheat the oven to 400°F/200°C/Gas Mark 6.

Discard any mussels with broken shells or any that do not shut immediately when sharply tapped. Put mussels in a pan along with wine, ¾ cup/175 ml water, shallot, herbs, and a pinch of salt. Cover and cook over high heat, shaking the pan occasionally, for 4–5 minutes, until the shells have opened.

Remove pan from heat and lift out mussels with a slotted spoon. Discard any that remain closed. Divide mussels on the half shells, open side up, among 6 individual ovenproof plates.

To make garlic and parsley butter, beat butter with garlic and parsley until thoroughly combined.

Using a round-bladed knife, place a little of the flavored butter on each mussel, covering it well. Put dishes in the oven for just 3 minutes, until garlic and parsley butter has melted. Serve hot.

# Salt Cod with Garlic

*Serves 6*
*Cook time: 30 minutes (plus soaking time)*

— 1 lb 2 oz/500 g salt cod, flaked
— 1 cup plus 2 tablespoons/275 ml
   sunflower oil
— 1 large onion, finely chopped
— 2 tablespoons olive oil
— 3–4 cloves garlic, finely chopped
— 3.5 oz/100 g jarred roasted red
   peppers, cut into strips

Put salt cod in a container and cover with water. Let soak overnight in the refrigerator.

Drain cod and pat dry. Cut skin into fine strips with kitchen scissors.

Heat sunflower oil in a Dutch oven (casserole) over medium heat. Add onion and garlic and cook, stirring occasionally, for about 5 minutes, or until very soft and translucent.

Heat olive oil in a small frying pan over low heat. Add peppers and cook, stirring occasionally, for 5 minutes.

Add cod and strips of skin to Dutch oven and cook for 10 minutes, shaking the pan occasionally, to release the gelatin. Add sautéed peppers. Mix well and cook, uncovered, over high heat, stirring often, for about 15 minutes, or until cooked through and browned.

Fish and Shellfish

# Porgy Baked with Garlic, Parsley, and Vinegar

*Serves 6*
*Cook time: 25 minutes*

— 1 cup/250 ml olive oil
— 1 large potato, thinly sliced
— salt
— 1 whole porgy (sea bream) or snapper
  (about 3 ¼ lb/1.5 kg), trimmed, scaled,
  and cleaned
— 2–3 large fennel fronds
— 3 tablespoons white wine vinegar
— 3 cloves garlic, finely chopped
— 1 tablespoon chopped parsley

Preheat the oven to 375°F/190°C/Gas Mark 5.

Heat oil in a frying pan over medium heat. Add potato slices and cook, turning occasionally, for about 6 minutes, or until softened but not browned. Remove with a slotted spatula (fish slice), lightly season with salt and put into a large ovenproof dish. Reserve the oil.

Season fish inside and out with salt and reshape. Put one of the fennel fronds in the cavity and put fish in the on top of the potatoes. Put a fennel frond underneath the fish and place the other on top. Pour 2 tablespoons of reserved oil over fish and bake for about 8 minutes.

Remove dish from oven and increase the oven temperature to 425°F/220°C/Gas Mark 7. Remove and discard fennel. Carefully pour half the vinegar inside the cavity, then sprinkle in half the garlic and half the parsley. Close fish, pour remaining vinegar over it and sprinkle with remaining garlic and parsley. Return to the oven for about 8 minutes, or until the flesh flakes easily, and serve hot, straight from the dish.

*Rodajas de merluza en salsa verde*

# Hake Steaks in Green Sauce

*Serves 6*
*Cook time: 30 minutes*

— 4 tablespoons olive oil
— 1 onion, chopped
— 1 clove garlic
— 2–3 sprigs parsley, plus 1 tablespoon very finely chopped parsley
— 1 tablespoon all-purpose (plain) flour
— 6 thick hake or whiting steaks (about 7 oz/200 g) each
— 1 cup (4 oz/120 g) canned peas, drained (optional)
— 1–2 eggs, hard-boiled (see page 230), chopped (optional)
— salt and pepper

Heat oil in a frying pan over medium heat. Add onion and cook, stirring, for 3 minutes, or until softened and translucent.

Meanwhile, crush garlic with parsley sprigs and a pinch of salt in a mortar.

Stir flour into the frying pan and cook, stirring, for 2 minutes. Gradually stir in 2 scant cups/450 ml water, a little at a time. Cook, stirring, for 3–5 minutes. Stir 2 tablespoons of the sauce into the garlic mixture, mix well and then return the garlic mixture to the frying pan. Pass sauce through a food mill or push through a coarse sieve into a flameproof dish.

Lightly season fish with salt and add to the dish. The sauce should just cover them, but if not, add a little more water. Lightly season with pepper, sprinkle with chopped parsley and add peas (if using). Cook, covered, over medium heat, gently shaking the dish, for 8–10 minutes. Taste and adjust the seasoning, if necessary. If desired, garnish with hard-boiled eggs. Serve hot.

Salmonetes al horno envueltos en papel

# Red Mullet Cooked en Papillote

*Serves 6*
*Cook time: 25 minutes*

— 6 whole red mullet or snapper (about 7 oz/200 g each), scaled and cleaned
— salt
— 6 tablespoons olive oil
— ½ teaspoon mixed dried herbs
— 6 sprigs thyme or fennel fronds
— 1 large onion, very finely chopped

Preheat the oven to 350°F/180°C/Gas Mark 4.

Cut out 6 squares of foil or parchment (baking) paper at least 2 inches/5 cm longer than the fish in one direction. Then fold the squares in half and cut into heart shapes (like making a valentine). Season fish inside and out with salt. Open the hearts and brush with some of the oil. Brush both sides of each fish with oil and place each fish, with the tail pointing down, along one edge of the sheet. Sprinkle dried herbs over the fish or put a fresh herb sprig into each cavity. Divide onion among them, then fold foil or paper in half over the fish and seal the edges. [If you use parchment (baking) paper, it might require a shorter cooking time than foil.]

Put the parcels on a baking sheet and bake for about 15 minutes. Serve fish in a dish with the parcels half open.

Note: This dish has the advantage that the fish can wait quite some time before being served without drying out. Also, the smell of fish is not so strong.

# Baked Sardines Stuffed with Spinach

*Serves 6*
*Cook time: 30 minutes*

— 7 tablespoons (100 g) butter
— 3 ¼ lb/1.5 kg spinach, coarse stems trimmed, blanched
— salt
— 3¼ lb/1.5 kg large fresh sardines or sprats, scaled, cleaned, and boned
— 4 tablespoons olive oil
— 2 tablespoons breadcrumbs

Preheat the oven to 350°F/180°C/Gas Mark 4. Melt 6 tablespoons (80 g) butter in a frying pan over medium heat. Add spinach and cook, stirring occasionally, for 5 minutes. Season to taste with salt. Remove from heat and keep warm.

Put fish on a work surface, skin side down. Lightly season with salt and divide the spinach among them, then roll up the fish. Pour oil into a 9 x 13-inch/23 x 33 cm baking dish, making sure that the base is covered. Put rolled-up fish into the dish in a single layer, sprinkle with the breadcrumbs and dot with the remaining 1 tablespoon (15 g) butter. Bake for 15 minutes, until cooked through. Serve hot, straight from the dish.

Truchas con jamón (a la Navarra)

# Navarra-Style Trout with Ham

*Serves 6*
*Cook time: 25 minutes*

— 6 trout (about 9 oz/250 g each), scaled
  and cleaned
— 6 thin slices Serrano ham
— 2 cups Tomato Sauce (page 231) or
  purchased
— 1 large red bell pepper, cut into strips
— generous 3 cups/750 ml sunflower oil
— generous ⅓ cup (50 grams) all-
  purpose (plain) flour
— salt

Season trout inside and out with salt and let stand for about 10 minutes. Place a slice of ham inside the cavity of each fish and close the cavity with a toothpick (cocktail stick).

Put tomato sauce and bell pepper in a saucepan and simmer over medium-low heat for 15 minutes, stirring occasionally.

Meanwhile, heat oil in a frying pan over high heat. Coat the trout in flour, shaking off any excess, add to the hot oil, in batches if necessary, and cook until golden brown. Transfer to the serving dish and serve hot with tomato sauce on the side.

# Fisherman's Cold Spider Crab

*Serves 2*
*Cook time: 30 minutes*

— ¾ cup/175 ml white wine vinegar
— 10 black peppercorns
— 3 bay leaves
— salt
— 2 spider crabs (mud crabs)
— 11 oz/300 g hake fillet
— 1 tablespoon white wine
— 1 thick slice onion
— 3 hard-boiled egg yolks
— ¼ teaspoon ground mustard
— juice of 1 lemon
— 4 tablespoons sunflower oil

Pour 5 quarts/5 L water into a saucepan, add vinegar, peppercorns, 2 bay leaves, and a generous pinch of salt and bring to a boil over high heat. Add crabs, cover, return to boil, and cook for 8 minutes. Drain and set aside to cool.

Meanwhile, put hake in a saucepan, add water to cover, along with remaining bay leaf, wine, onion, and a pinch of salt. Bring to a boil; remove from heat. Lift out hake, remove and discard skin and bones, and flake the flesh.

Once crabs are cool, open carefully without breaking back shells. Remove and discard gills. Take out white meat from the body and the legs and cut into pieces. Scoop brown meat into a bowl; reserve any roe from a hen crab. Wash and dry back shells and set aside.

Pound the brown meat, roe (if available), hard-boiled egg yolks, mustard, and lemon juice in a mortar. Gradually whisk in soil, and season with salt. Combine hake, white crab meat, and sauce. Divide mixture between 2 reserved crab shells. Refrigerate until ready to serve.

# Meat and Poultry

Traditionally, meat was a luxury ingredient. From slaughtered pigs, the Spanish would make sausages, hams, and bacon to last throughout the year, while the meat was used sparingly as a flavoring, like in Migas. Scarcity and value of meat ensured that virtually every part of the animal was used to its fullest potential. Game dishes were popular in the winter as they came out of hunting expeditions, and became the basis of some of Spain's most creative dishes, like Cornish Game Hens in Potato Nests. As Spain has grown more prosperous, and the quality of meat has improved, meat as a centerpiece has become more commonplace with dishes such as Tenderloin Steaks with Port and Mustard Sauce, as well as Pork Chops with Honey, Lemon, and Curry Powder.

# Tenderloin Steaks with Port and Mustard Sauce

*Serves 6*
*Cook time: 15 minutes*

— 6 beef tenderloin (fillet) steaks
 (about 5 oz/150 g each)
— 4 tablespoons olive oil
— salt
— ½ teaspoon ground mustard
— 5 tablespoons port

Brush both sides of the steaks with a little oil and season with salt. Heat remaining oil in a frying pan over high heat. Cook steaks for 2–4 minutes per side, until done to your liking. Transfer to a serving dish and keep warm.

Stir mustard and port into the frying pan and cook for 2–3 minutes until slightly thickened. Pour sauce over steaks and serve hot.

# Pork Chops with Honey, Lemon, and Curry Powder

*Serves 6*
*Cook time: 30 minutes*

— 6 tablespoons olive oil
— 6 tablespoons mild honey
— 3 tablespoons fresh lemon juice
— 1 ½ teaspoons curry powder
— salt
— 6 (4 oz/115 g each) boneless pork
    chops (about ¾-inch/2 cm thick),
    at room temperature
— sunflower oil

Mix together olive oil, honey, lemon juice, curry powder, and a pinch of salt in a nonreactive dish. Add chops, turning to coat, and set aside to marinate for 10 minutes.

Add enough sunflower oil to a frying pan to generously cover the base of the pan and heat over medium heat. Reserving the marinade, drain chops. Working in batches, add chops to the pan and cook for 3–5 minutes on each side until just a touch pink in the center. Remove from pan and keep warm.

Pour reserved marinade into the frying pan and bring to a boil, then pour over the chops and serve hot.

# Meatballs

*Serves 4-6*
*Cook time: 30 minutes*

— 1 lb 2 oz/500 g ground (minced) beef
— 1 sprig parsley, chopped
— 1 clove garlic, very finely chopped
— 1 egg, lightly beaten
— 4 tablespoons breadcrumbs
— 3 tablespoons white wine
— salt
— 5 tablespoons all-purpose (plain) flour
— generous 2 cups/500 ml sunflower oil
— Basic Tomato Sauce (page 231)
— 1 small pinch saffron threads

Put beef, parsley, garlic, egg, breadcrumbs, wine, and a pinch of salt in a bowl and mix well. Shape the mixture into small balls, rolling them between the palms of your hands. Lightly coat the meatballs in flour.

Heat oil in a large frying pan over medium heat. Working in batches, add meatballs to the hot oil and cook, turning frequently, until golden brown all over, 5 to 7 minutes. Using a slotted spoon, transfer meatballs to a large pan, arranging them in a single layer.

Meanwhile, bring the tomato sauce to a simmer in a saucepan over medium-low heat.

Pour tomato sauce over the meatballs. Crush saffron threads in a mortar, then stir in a scant ½ cup/100 ml water and pour mixture into the pan. Simmer meatballs in the sauce for 10–15 minutes, then serve.

Note: You can also make the meatballs with ground veal or a mixture of ground beef and pork. Simmer veal meatballs for 10 minutes only.

Solomillitos de cerdo al vino

# Pork Fillets in Wine

*Serves 8*
*Cook time: 30 minutes*

— 1 lb 7 oz (640 g) pork tenderloin
   (fillet), cut into 8 slices
— salt and pepper
— 1 tablespoon potato starch (flour)
— 2 tablespoons (30 g) butter
— generous 2 cups (500 ml) good
   red wine
— 2 shallots, finely chopped
— 2 tablespoons Tomato Sauce,
   homemade (page 231) or purchased
— 1 teaspoon beef bouillon granules

Preheat the oven to 350°F/180°C/Gas Mark 4.
Season pork slices on both sides with salt and
pepper, then coat them in potato starch and shake
off any excess.

Heat butter in a Dutch oven (casserole)
over high heat. Add pork and cook for 2 minutes,
turning to brown both sides. Add wine, shallots,
tomato sauce, beef bouillon, and a scant ½ cup
(100 ml) water to the dish. Season with salt and
pepper. Cover dish, transfer to the oven, and bake
for 15 minutes.

Remove pork fillets and cover them with foil to
keep warm. Place pan on the stove over high heat
and cook for 5 minutes, to allow the sauce to
thicken. Remove from heat, return pork to the
pan, and let stand for 2 minutes before serving.

# Migas

*Serves 6*
*Cook time: 30 minutes*

— 1 lb 2 oz/500 g day-old white bread, cubed
— 1¼ cups (300 ml) olive oil
— 7 oz/200 g semi-salted pork belly (pork side), cubed
— 7 oz/200 g Spanish chorizo, casings removed, sliced
— 3 cloves garlic, sliced
— 1 teaspoon paprika
— salt

Soak bread in 2 tablespoons of water while you prepare the recipe.

Meanwhile, heat the oil in a Dutch oven (casserole) or a large frying pan over medium-hight heat. Add pork and pan-fry for about 5 minutes, or until browned and cooked through. Remove using a slotted spoon and set aside.

Pan-fry chorizo in the same oil, about 10 minutes, then remove and set aside.

Finally, pan-fry garlic in the same oil, until golden brown.

Add bread and paprika and continue stirring for 15 minutes so that the "crumbs" stay loose and become crisp. Serve with chorizo and pork belly. Migas is also excellent with fried eggs.

Meat and Poultry

# Cornish Game Hens in Potato Nests

*Serves 6*
*Cook time: 30 minutes*

— 3 (1¼ lb/565 g) Cornish game hens,
   split lengthwise
— salt
— 4 tablespoons (2 oz/50 g) lard
— 6 slices (rashers) bacon, halved
— about 3 quarts/3 L sunflower oil,
   for deep-frying
— 2¼ lb/1 kg potatoes, thinly sliced,
   then cut into fine straws

Preheat the oven to 475°F/190°C/Gas Mark 5.

Season cavities of the hens with salt. Set a wire rack in a rimmed baking sheet and set hens skin side up on the rack. Rub their skin with a little lard and drape each with a piece of bacon. Roast for 25 minutes, or until tender.

Meanwhile, heat sunflower oil in a deep-fryer or deep saucepan to 350°–375°F/180°–190°C, or until a cube of day-old bread browns in 30 seconds. Divide potato straws into 6 equal amounts. Spread one amount over the base and slightly up the sides of a wire frying basket and lower into the hot oil, pressing it together. Cook for about 3 minutes, or until golden brown, then drain. Repeat with remaining potato straws to make 6 nests.

Put a roasted hen half, breast side up, in each potato nest.

Stir 3–4 tablespoons hot water into the baking sheet and set over medium heat, scraping up any bits from the base of the pan, for a few minutes. Pour into a sauceboat and serve hot with hens.

# Chicken Brochettes with Spices and Honey

*Makes 6*
*Cook time: 30 minutes*

— juice of 4 lemons, strained
— 4 teaspoons curry powder
— 2 teaspoons paprika
— 2 teaspoons ground cumin
— 2 teaspoons ground ginger
— 1 star anise
— 3 tablespoons honey
— 1¼ lb/565 g boneless, skinless
    chicken or turkey breast, cubed
— 1 red bell pepper, cut into chunks
— 1 onion, cut into large pieces
— Olive oil, for brushing the pan
— Cooked basmati rice, to serve

Pour lemon juice into a large nonreactive bowl and stir in curry powder, paprika, cumin, ginger, and star anise.

Heat honey in a small saucepan, then stir in the lemon-spice mixture. Pour mixture back into the bowl, add chicken cubes, and stir to coat, ensuring all the pieces are well covered. Let chicken marinate for about 10 minutes.

Fill 6 skewers by alternating cubes of meat with pieces of pepper and onion (reserve the marinade). Heat a ridged cast-iron pan or frying pan over very high heat until you can feel the heat rising. Brush the frying pan with some olive oil. Add brochettes and cook for about 15 minutes, turning occasionally and basting with reserved marinade, until the meat is tender and juices run clear when you insert the tip of a sharp knife. Set brochettes aside and keep warm.

Pour the remaining marinade into the frying pan, bring to a boil, and let caramelize before pouring it over the brochettes. Serve with basmati rice.

# Chicken Livers with Grapes

*Serves 4*
*Cook time: 20 minutes*

— 1 tablespoon (15 g) butter
— 3 tablespoons sunflower oil
— 1 lb 5 oz (600 g) chicken livers, trimmed
— 2 shallots, finely chopped
— 4 tablespoons rum, brandy, or Madeira
— 14 oz/400 g seedless white grapes (peeled, if desired)
— salt and pepper

Melt butter with oil in a large frying pan over low heat Add chicken livers and pan-fry, turning occasionally, for about 8 minutes, or until they are golden brown on the outside but not overcooked on the inside. Lift out with a slotted spoon, set aside, and keep warm.

Add shallots to remaining oil in the pan and pan-fry over low heat, stirring occasionally, for 3 minutes, or until softened but not colored. Increase heat to medium, pour in rum, brandy, or Madeira, and cook for 3 minutes, stirring constantly. Add grapes, reduce heat a little, and allow to warm through. Return the livers to the frying pan just long enough to heat up and season with salt and pepper. Serve livers in a warmed dish, surrounded by grapes and covered with the juices from the frying pan.

# Chicken and Bell Pepper Empanada

*Makes 1 empanada*
*Cook time: 30 minutes*

— olive oil, for frying
— 14 oz/400 g boneless, skinless chicken breast, cut into 2 ½-inch/6 cm cubes
— salt
— 1 sheet refrigerated pie dough (shortcrust pastry)
— 3 cups Tomato Sauce (page 231) or purchased
— 1 cup chopped jarred roasted red peppers
— 1 egg, lightly beaten

Preheat the oven to 475°F/190°C/Gas Mark 5.

Heat a little oil in a frying pan and add chicken. Cook for 10 minutes, or until cooked through. Season with a little salt.

Make sure your dough is rolled out into a large (12-inch / 30-cm) round. Spread tomato sauce over the dough and scatter the chicken on top. Top with a layer of roasted peppers. Fold one side of the dough over the filling; crimp the edges together.

Transfer empanada to a baking sheet. Brush dough with the beaten egg and bake for 20–25 minutes, until puffed up and golden brown. Serve warm, sliced into pieces.

# Desserts

Traditionally, the sweet course in Spain is a piece of
fresh fruit or a handful of dried fruit and nuts, with a
glass of muscatel wine. It is still a Northern Spanish
penchant to serve a bowl of fresh cheese drizzled with
honey. These simple plates make classy finishes to a
meal and require little effort, but it is worth trying your
hand at some cooked desserts too: hot lemon donuts
dredged in sugar, a tender jam and cream-filled sponge
roll known as *Brazo de gitano*, and figs stewed in red
wine and spices.

# Lemon Doughnuts

*Makes about 23*
*Cook time: 30 minutes*

— 2 eggs
— 8 tablespoons (3.5 oz/100 g) lard,
  melted
— ⅔ cup (160 ml) milk
— Finely grated zest of 1 small lemon
— 2 tablespoons anisette liqueur
— 1 cup (235 g) superfine (caster) sugar
— 5½ cups (690 g) all-purpose (plain)
  flour, plus extra for dusting
— ½ teaspoon baking powder or baking
  soda (bicarbonate of soda)
— sunflower oil, for deep-frying
— powdered (icing) sugar, for dusting

Put eggs, lard, milk, lemon zest, anisette, and sugar in a bowl and stir until combined. Stir in 2 cups flour and baking powder. Continue adding more flour, a little at a time, until the dough comes away from the sides of the bowl (you may not need all of the flour).

With floured hands, form the dough into little rolls about ⅝-inch/1.5 cm thick.

Heat oil in a deep-fryer or deep saucepan to 300°–325°F/150°–160°C, or until a cube of day-old bread browns in 45 seconds.

Working in batches, carefully add doughnuts to hot oil and cook until puffed up, then turn up the heat and cook until golden brown. Remove doughnuts from oil with a slotted spoon, drain well, and dust with sugar. Repeat with the remaining batter.

# Roulade

*Serves 8*
*Cook time: 30 minutes*

— butter, for greasing
— 4 tablespoons all-purpose (plain) flour
— 2 tablespoons potato starch (flour)
— 1 teaspoon baking powder
— pinch of vanilla powder or a few drops of vanilla extract
— 3 eggs, separated
— 1 egg white
— salt
— 5 tablespoons superfine (caster) sugar
— 2 cups jam of your choice
— 1 cup heavy (double) cream, whipped into soft peaks
— powdered (icing) sugar, to decorate

Preheat the oven to 375°F/190°C/Gas Mark 5. Grease a 15 x 10 inch/38 x 25 cm jelly-roll pan (Swiss roll tin) with butter. Line the base with wax (greaseproof) paper and grease the paper with butter.

Sift flour, potato starch, baking powder, and vanilla powder (if using) into a bowl.

Whisk 4 egg whites with a pinch of salt in a dry bowl until stiff peaks form. Add yolks and vanilla extract (if using), then superfine (caster) sugar, and the flour mixture, a spoonful at a time. Spoon into the prepared pan and bake for 6–7 minutes, until firm and lightly browned or until a toothpick (cocktail stick) inserted into the center of the cake comes out clean.

Spread a wrung-out tea towel on a work surface and turn the cake out onto it. Discard the wax paper and refrigerate for 5 minutes.

Spread jam and whipped cream over cake and, using the tea towel, roll it up. Cover and cool. Before serving, trim off the cake ends and top with powdered sugar.

Desserts

# Apple Fritters

*Serves 4*
*Cook time: 30 minutes*

*For the batter*
— 2½ cups (300 g) all-purpose (plain) flour
— salt
— 3 tablespoons white wine
— 3 tablespoons sunflower oil
— 1 tablespoon superfine (caster) sugar, plus extra for coating
— 1¾ cups/440 ml milk
— ½ teaspoon baking powder

*For the apples*
— 4 apples, peeled and cut into ¼-inch/0.5 cm-thick rings
— juice of ½ lemon
— 3 tablespoons sugar, plus more for coating
— 4 tablespoons rum
— sunflower oil, for deep-frying

To make the batter, sift flour with a pinch of salt into a bowl. Make a well in the center, pour in wine and oil and add sugar. Mix well, then stir in milk. Cover and let rest for 10 minutes while you prepare apples.

Toss the apple slices in lemon juice to prevent discoloration. Mix together sugar, rum and 1 cup/250 ml water in a large saucepan. Bring to a simmer over medium-high heat. Add apples and simmer for about 3 minutes, or until soft but not falling apart. Drain well and pat dry.

Heat oil in a deep-fryer or deep saucepan to 350°–375°F/180°–190°C, or until a cube of day-old bread browns in 30 seconds.

Stir baking powder into batter. One at a time, dip the apple slices into batter and add to hot oil, frying in batches, and cook until golden brown. Remove with a slotted spoon and drain well, then coat fritters in superfine sugar while they are still hot. Put fritters on a serving dish and keep warm while cooking the remaining batches. Serve hot.

# Fresh Fruit Soup with Cava

*Serves 4*
*Cook time: 30 minutes*

— 1 small pineapple, peeled, cored, and
  cut into ½-inch/1.25 cm pieces, juice
  reserved
— 20 fresh lychees (180 g)
— 1¾ cups (11 oz/300 g) raspberries
— 2 tablespoons plus 1 teaspoon (80 g)
  light brown sugar
— 2½ cups/600 ml cava or other
  sparkling white wine, chilled
— 4 fresh mint leaves

*To serve*
— juice of ½ lemon
— superfine (caster) sugar

Put pineapple in a large bowl. Peel, halve, and pit lychees and add them to the pineapple along with raspberries. Stir in sugar and chill in the refrigerator for 25 minutes. Just before serving, pour reserved pineapple juice and sparkling wine over the fruit.

Meanwhile, to prepare the glasses for serving the fruit soup. Brush the rims of 4 large goblets or water glasses with lemon juice, then dip them into a saucer of superfine sugar to frost the rims.

Spoon fruit and juices into prepared glasses. Garnish with mint leaves.

Note: You can make this with oranges instead of pineapple. Cut off orange peels, removing all traces of pith, then cut the segments from between the membranes and chop. Do this over a dish to collect the juices. Squeeze any juice out of the membranes. Pour reserved juice over the fruit with the wine, just before serving.

# Churros

*Makes about 25*
*Cook time: 25 minutes*

— 1⅓ cups (175 g) all-purpose (plain) flour
— sunflower oil, for deep-frying
— powdered (icing) sugar, for dredging
— salt

Pour 1½ cups/350 ml water into a saucepan, add a pinch of salt and bring to a boil. Tip in flour all at once and cook, stirring constantly, until the mixture comes away from the sides of the pan. Remove pan from heat and set aside to cool.

Heat oil in a deep-fryer or deep saucepan to 350°–375°F/180°–190°C, or until a cube of day-old bread browns in 30 seconds.

Put cooled dough into a churro maker or a large plastic bag with one of its corners snipped off and squeeze out the churros, cutting them into 8-inch (20-cm) strips with a sharp knife as the dough is pushed out. Working in batches, carefully add churros immediately to the hot oil.(Alternatively, spoon cooled dough into a pastry bag fitted with a star tip and pipe directly into the hot oil, cutting churros to the required length with a sharp knife.) When the strips of fried dough are golden brown all over, remove with a slotted spoon, drain well, dredge with powdered (icing) sugar and serve hot.

# Catalan Cream

*Serves 6*
*Cook time: 15 minutes (plus chilling time)*

— 4¼ cups/1 L milk
— ½ cup plus 3 tablespoons (135 g)
    superfine (caster) sugar
— strips of zest from 1 lemon
— 8 egg yolks
— 2 tablespoons potato starch (potato
    flour) or cornstarch (corn flour)

Pour milk into a saucepan, add 4 tablespoons sugar and lemon zest and bring just to a boil.

Meanwhile, beat egg yolks with 2 tablespoons sugar and potato starch.

Gradually whisk hot milk into egg yolks, then pour custard back into the saucepan. Reduce heat and cook, stirring constantly, for about 5 minutes, or until thickened. Strain into a serving dish or individual dishes and set aside to cool, refrigerate for at least 1 hour.

Just before serving, sprinkle remaining 5 tablespoons sugar on top and use a crème brûlée torch to caramelize it.

Note: Crema catalana is the best-known Spanish dessert and is said by some to be the predecessor of France's crème brûlée.

# Orange Souffles

*Serves 4*
*Cook time: 30 minutes*

— 4 large oranges
— ½ cup (100 g) superfine (caster) sugar
— 2 heaped tablespoons cornstarch (corn flour)
— 3 tablespoons Cointreau, Curaçao, or other orange liqueur
— 2 eggs, separated
— 1 egg white
— salt

Cut a thin slice off the base of each orange so that it stands flat. Cut a slice off the top and squeeze out the juice without damaging the "shells." Scoop out and discard the pulp on the orange peel and reserve the shells.

Set up a large bowl of ice water. Measure out 1½ cups/350 ml orange juice and pour into a saucepan. Stir in sugar. Mix cornstarch to a paste with 5 tablespoons water in a bowl.

Heat orange juice over medium heat and when bubbles begin to appear around the edges of the pan, stir in the cornstarch mixture and cook, stirring constantly, for 3 minutes. Remove pan from heat, set in the ice bath, stirring constantly to prevent a skin forming and to cool it down faster.

Preheat the broiler (grill). Stir liqueur into the orange juice mixture, then beat in egg yolks. Whisk 3 egg whites with a pinch of salt in a clean, dry bowl until stiff peaks form, then gently fold into egg yolk mixture.

Divide mixture among the orange shells and broil (grill) for 6–8 minutes. Serve hot.

# Chocolate Mousse with Ladyfingers

*Serves 6–8*
*Cook time: 30 minutes (plus chilling time)*

— 3.5 oz/100 g dark chocolate, broken
  into pieces
— 3 tablespoons milk
— 12 tablespoons (6 oz/175 g) butter,
  at room temperature, plus extra for
  greasing
— 3 eggs, separated
— 6 tablespoons superfine (caster) sugar
— 1 egg white
— salt
— 3–4 tablespoons rum
— 40 ladyfingers (sponge fingers)
— whipped cream, to serve (optional)

Gently heat chocolate and milk in a saucepan until the chocolate melts. Remove from heat and stir in butter, one tablespoon (15 g) at a time.

Beat egg yolks with 3 tablespoons sugar, then add melted chocolate mixture. Stir to combine. Whisk 4 egg whites with a pinch of salt in a dry bowl until stiff peaks form. Gently fold egg whites into chocolate mixture. Chill mousse while you prepare the ladyfingers.

Meanwhile, butter an 8-inch/20 cm round cake pan. Mix rum, remaining sugar, and 1½cups/350 ml water, in a shallow dish. Dip half the ladyfingers in mixture and layer them on the bottom of the pan. Line the sides with trimmed, dipped ladyfingers. Spoon half of mousse into pan; alternate with dipped ladyfingers, remainng mousse, and another layer of ladyfingers. Top with a greased plate slightly smaller than the diameter of the pan so it rests inside the tin; place a light weight on top and chill for 5 hours. To serve, remove plate, run a knife around the edge of pan, and turn mousse out onto a serving dish. If desired, serve with whipped cream.

# Fruit Gelatin (Jelly)

*Serves 6*
*Cook time: 30 minutes (plus chilling time)*

— 1 lb 2 oz/500 g cut-up mixed fresh
   fruit, such as bananas, apples,
   peaches, plums, grapes, strawberries,
   or raspberries
— 3 tablespoons rum or brandy
— ½ cup plus 2 tablespoons (125 g)
   superfine (caster) sugar
— 1 cup/250 ml fresh orange juice
— 1 packet (2½ teaspoons) unflavored
   powdered gelatin

Make this dessert the night before you intend to
serve it. Put fruit in a bowl, pour rum or brandy
over them and leave to macerate, stirring
occasionally while you prepare the recipe.

Pour ⅔ cup/150 ml water into a saucepan, stir in
sugar, and cook over medium heat for about
4 minutes to make a syrup.

Meanwhile, pour orange juice into a bowl,
sprinkle gelatin over the top and let soften
for 5 minutes.

Stir the hot syrup into the orange juice, mixing
until the gelatin has completely dissolved. Pour
in the liquid to a depth of about ¾ inch/2 cm and
chill in the freezer until set, about 25 minutes.

Arrange the fruit on top and pour in remaining
liquid. Chill in the refrigerator for several hours
before serving. Turn the dessert out of the mold
to serve.

# Fig Compote with Red Wine and Spices

*Serves 4–6*
*Cook time: 25 minutes*

— 3 tablespoons red wine
— 2 large strips orange zest
— 3 tablespoons superfine (caster) sugar
— 1 cinnamon stick
— 6 cloves
— 1 sprig mint
— 24 small or 12 large fresh figs, peeled

Combine wine and a generous ½ cup/135 ml water in a saucepan. Add orange zest, sugar, cinnamon, cloves, and mint and simmer for 5 minutes. Add figs and cook over low heat for 6 minutes. Lift out figs with a slotted spoon and put them into a serving bowl.

Simmer the cooking liquid for another 15 minutes. Strain it into a bowl, reserving the orange zest, and set aside to cool. Cut orange zest into very thin slivers and add to the figs. Pour sauce over the figs and chill in the refrigerator.

# Santiago Torte

*Serves 6*
*Cook time: 30 minutes*

— 2 sticks plus 2 tablespoons (9 oz/250 g)
   butter, at room temperature, plus extra
   for greasing
— 8 eggs
— 2 ½ cups (500 g) superfine (caster)
   sugar
— 3 cups plus 3 tablespoons (400 g)
   all-purpose (plain) flour
— 5 cups (500 g) almond meal/flour
   (ground almonds)
— grated zest of 1 lemon
— powdered (icing) sugar, to decorate

Preheat the oven to 375°F/190°C/Gas Mark 5.
Grease an 8-inch (20-cm) cake pan with butter.

Beat eggs with superfine sugar in a bowl until pale
and fluffy, then beat in flour, butter, and 1
cup/250 ml water. Mix well, then stir in ground
almonds and lemon zest.

Pour batter into the prepared pan and
bake for about 20 minutes. Increase oven
temperature to 425°F/220°C/Gas Mark 7 and
bake 10 minutes, or until a toothpick (cocktail
stick) inserted in the center comes out clean.

Let torte cool in the pan, then turn it out. Dust
with powdered sugar. For an attractive effect, cut
out a simple cardboard stencil, such as a star, and
hold this over the torte when you decorate it with
powdered sugar.

Note: The torte can also be dusted with
cocoa powder.

Desserts

# Traditional Christmas Cookies (Biscuits)

*Makes 8–9 dozen*
*Cook time: 25 minutes*

— butter, for greasing
— 5½ cups (750 g) all-purpose (plain) flour, plus extra for dusting
— 3 tablespoons superfine (caster) sugar
— 1¾ cups (14 oz/400 g) lard
— juice of ½ lemon
— powdered (icing) sugar and ground cinnamon, to decorate

Preheat the oven to 350°F/150°C/Gas Mark 2. Grease a baking sheet with butter.

Sift flour onto a counter, make a well in the center and add sugar, lard, and lemon juice. Knead together until the dough is smooth, then allow to rest for 5 minutes in the refrigerator.

Using a floured rolling pin, roll out dough on a lightly floured surface to about ⅜ inch/8 mm thick. Stamp out small rounds or ovals with a 2-inch/5 cm cookie (biscuit) cutter (some people also like to make a hole in the center of each one). Put cutouts on the prepared baking sheet and bake for about 15 minutes, until set but not browned. Remove from the oven and sprinkle with powdered sugar and ground cinnamon.

# Basic Recipes

Spanish cuisine is rich in flavor, yet remarkably unfussy
and simple to create. Recipes such as homemade
mayonnaise, hard-boiled eggs, tomato sauce, and fried
bread, are the kind of staples the Spanish always keep
in their pantry to effortlessly throw together meals,
whether for a weekday dinner on a busy night or to
entertain. They cost little to make and elevate your
cooking as if you spent all day in the kitchen. That
is Spanish cooking in a nutshell: uncomplicated and,
above all, made for sharing.

Mayonesa

# Mayonnaise

*Makes about 1 cup*
*Cook time: 10 minutes*

— 1 egg yolk, at room
temperature
— 1 tablespoon white wine
vinegar or lemon juice,
strained
— salt
— generous 1 cup/250 ml
sunflower oil

Put egg yolk in a bowl with 1½ teaspoons of the vinegar or lemon juice and a small pinch of salt. Stir lightly with a whisk or fork and then gradually whisk in oil, 1–2 teaspoons at a time, until about one-quarter has been added.

Whisk in remaining oil in a slow, steady stream. Add remaining vinegar or lemon juice, then taste and adjust the seasoning. It is a good idea to make the mayonnaise in a cool place and store it in the refrigerator.

Huevos duros

# Hard-Boiled Eggs

*Makes 2 eggs*
*Cook time: 10 minutes*

— 2 eggs

Set up a bowl of ice and water.

Place eggs in a saucepan, generously cover with water, and bring to a boil.

Immediately remove from heat, cover, and let stand for 10 minutes. Transfer eggs to the ice bath and let cool before peeling. Unpeeled eggs will keep refrigerated for up to 1 week.

Salsa de tomate

# Tomato Sauce

*Makes about 7 cups/1.75 l*
*Cook time: 15 minutes*

— 3 tablespoons olive oil
— 4 tablespoons chopped onion
— 3¼ lb/1.5 kg tomatoes, seeded and diced or 2 (28 oz/795 g) cans tomatoes
— 1 teaspoon sugar
— salt

Heat oil in a frying pan over low heat until shimmering. Add onion and cook, stirring occasionally until transluscent. Add tomatoes and cook (breaking the canned tomatoes up with the edge of a wooden spoon) for 10 minutes. Let cool slightly, then transfer to a food processor or blender and process to a puree. Add sugar and salt to taste.

Pan frito

# Fried Bread

— 1 cup (250 ml) olive oil
— 5 ounces (140 g) day-old bread, thinly sliced

Heat oil in a frying pan over medium heat. Add bread slices, in batches, and fry for 2 minutes, until golden brown on both sides. Remove with a slotted spatula and drain on paper towels.

# Cooking Time Index

# 5 minutes

# 10 minutes

# 15 minutes

# 20 minutes

# 25 minutes

# 30 minutes

# Index

Phaidon Press Limited
Regent's Wharf
All Saints Street
London N1 9PA

Phaidon Press Inc.
65 Bleecker Street
New York, NY 10012

www.phaidon.com

**RECIPE NOTES**

Some recipes include raw or very lightly cooked eggs. These should be avoided by the elderly, infants, pregnant women, convalescents, and anyone with an impaired immune system. Mushrooms should be wiped clean. Butter should always be unsalted. Eggs are assumed to be large. Milk is assumed to be whole (full-fat). When deep-frying, exercise a high level of caution when following recipes involving any potentially hazardous activity, including the use of high temperature and open flames. In particular, when deep-frying, add the food carefully to avoid splashing, wear long sleeves, and never leave the pan unattended.

3361405994266З

© 2016 Phaidon Press Limited
ISBN 978 0 7148 7113 4

*Quick and Easy Spanish Recipes* originates from *1080 Recetas de Cocina* first published in 1972 by Alianza Editorial, S.A and *The Book of Tapas*, first published in 2010 by Phaidon Press Limited.

A CIP catalogue record for this book is available from the British Library and the Library of Congress.

Commissioning Editor: Emily Takoudes
Project Editor: Olga Massov
Production Controller: Adela Cory
Design by atlas.
Photographs by Jason Lowe and Mauricio Salinas

Printed in Slovenia

The publishers would like to thank Simone and Inés Ortega, Pearl Jones, Cecilia Molinari, Kate Slate, Tara Stevens, and Gemma Wilson, for their contributions to the book.